D1805976

The CSFB Guide to
Yield Calculations In The International Bond & Money Markets

The CSFB Guide to
Yield Calculations In The International Bond & Money Markets

☐ **Structure**

☐ **Trends**

☐ **Analysis**

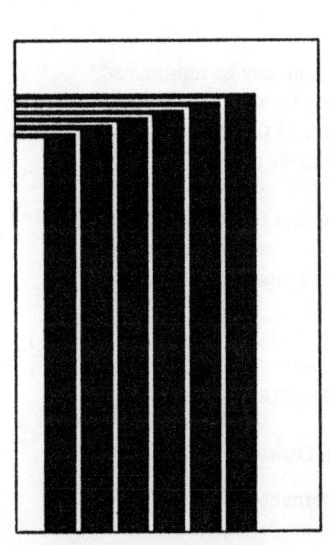

Credit Suisse First Boston

Probus Publishing Company
Chicago, Illinois

Library of Congress Cataloging in Publication Data

The CSFB guide to yield calculation in the International
    bond & money markets.

    1. Bonds. 2. Money market. I. Credit Suisse First
Boston. II. Title: Yield calculations in the Inter-
national bond & money markets.
HG4651.C74   1988   332.63'23   88-25457
ISBN 1-55738-023-6

Printed in the United States of America.

1 2 3 4 5 6 7 8 9 0

Contents

I   Summary

- Yield is the most widely used measure of the value to an investor of a fixed-interest security. However, surprisingly few people understand the principles, let alone the details, behind the calculation of yields.

- Many different methods of calculating yields are used in the different bond markets of the world. This makes direct comparison of the quoted yields for different securities across markets, or sometimes even within the same market, potentially misleading.

- It is possible to calculate yields in a consistent fashion which allows yield comparisons to be made safely. CSFB recommends a method of yield calculation that accounts for the precise times on which cash flows are received (see page 38).

- In order to calculate the yield of a fixed-interest security, certain market specific information must be known. For example, it is necessary to know which of the variety of methods of accrued interest calculation is used in the particular market.

- Duration and convexity are two quantities, related to yield, which provide a useful indication of the likely performance of a bond when interest rates change.

- Yield, duration and convexity can also be used for evaluating a portfolio of bonds.

An investor purchasing a fixed-interest security is acquiring a series of expected future cash flows.* The price he will pay reflects the market valuation of these future cash flows. However, price is not a useful figure for comparing the relative attractiveness of two securities unless they have exactly the same cash flows.

Yields do allow sensible comparisons to be made between two securities having different cash flows. Other things being equal, the security with the higher yield is the more attractive investment.

Unfortunately there are a number of different figures which are quoted in the markets, all of which are termed 'yield', and yet which are calculated in different ways. This can be misleading for the investor.

For example, a 9% U.S. Treasury bond bought for settlement on 1st May, 1986 at a price, including accrued interest, of $102.71 and maturity date 1st August, 1986 would have a quoted yield of 6.857%. A Federal Agency bond with identical coupon and maturity bought for the same price and settling on the same date would have a quoted yield of 6.971%, about 11 basis points higher. From the point of view of their cash flows the two bonds are equally attractive, yet their quoted yields are different.

Sections III and IV introduce the concept of yield for money market instruments and bonds and explain the various methods of calculation. Throughout the book, worked examples and the minimum of mathematics are used to illustrate the basic ideas. The general mathematical formulae for calculating yields are confined to the appendices.

---

*The valuation of Floating Rate Notes (FRNs) is outside the scope of this publication. For details see 'Floating Rate Notes: Methods of Analysis', CSFB Research, June 1986.

There are number of other measures related to yield which are used to evaluate bonds. Duration and convexity provide an indication of the likely performance of a bond when interest rates change. Section V describes the calculation of these quantities and shows how they are used in practice.

Section VI shows how yield, duration and convexity can be calculated for a portfolio of fixed-interest securities.

It is common practice to quote bond prices net of accrued interest. Since this accrued interest is added to the quoted price to determine the total price paid for a bond, it must be known in order to calculate the yield. The way in which accrued interest is calculated varies between markets. Section VII shows how to calculate accrued interest according to the various market conventions.

Other market conventions such as the relation of the settlement and value date to the trade date, and ex-dividend dates must also be known when calculating yields. These are described for a number of markets in section VIII.

In the past, the segregation of markets has led to different conventions for the calculation of yields. However, domestic markets around the world are being increasingly opened up to foreign investors. Therefore, there is a greater need for a method of yield calculation which can be applied in any market. CSFB recommends a consistent method of yield calculation which allows direct comparisons to be made between the yields of fixed-interest securities in different markets and of different types. The use of a consistent yield calculation method is particularly important when computing the average yield of a portfolio containing a variety of instruments.

Most money market instruments have maturities of less than one year and pay one lump sum at maturity. For this reason the calculation of their yields is generally much simpler than for bonds: straightforward simple interest is used.

Certificates of Deposit (CDs) which pay more than one coupon are, in terms of their pattern of cash flows, similar to bonds. However, a different method is generally used for CDs to relate price to yield.

Money market instruments are traded either on a discount basis or on a yield basis.

Instruments Traded on a Discount Basis

Treasury Bills, Bankers Acceptances and Commercial Paper are generally sold on the basis of a discount to par. The rate of discount, which is also known as the discount yield, is quoted at an annual rate on the basis of a 360 or 365 day year depending on the market. For example, a 360 day year is used in the U.S. market and a 365 day year in the U.K. market (see 'Market Details' for further information). The price is related to the rate of discount by the formula:

$$P = F \times \left(1 - \frac{R}{100} \times \frac{D_{sm}}{A_d}\right)$$

where:

P	= Price
F	= Face value
R	= Rate of discount %
D_{sm}	= Number of days from settlement to maturity
A_d	= Assumed number of days in a year for quoting discounts

Example

A U.S. Treasury Bill, which matures on 13th March, 1986, is bought for settlement on 20th February, 1986 at a rate of discount of 7.0%. There are 21 days from settlement to maturity. In the U.S. Treasury market discounts are quoted on the basis of a 360 day year. Therefore the price per $100 face value is:

$$P = 100 \times \left(1 - \frac{7.0}{100} \times \frac{21}{360}\right) = \$99.592$$

The rate of discount can be converted to a yield for comparison with money market instruments traded on a yield basis using the formula:

$$Y = \frac{100 \times R \times A_d}{(100 \times A_d - R \times D_{sm})} = 100\left(\frac{100}{P} - 1\right)\frac{A_y}{D_{sm}}$$

where:
Y = Yield %
R = Rate of discount %
D_{sm} = Number of days from settlement to maturity
A_d = Assumed number of days in a year for money market yields and discounts

Example
For the U.S. Treasury Bill in the previous example the yield is given by:

$$Y = \frac{100 \times 7.0 \times 360}{(100 \times 360 - 7.0 \times 21)} = 7.029\%$$

This figure could be directly compared with the yield quoted on, for example, a Certificate of Deposit (see page 10). Note that the yield is larger than the rate of discount; this is always the case.

Equivalent Bond Yields

In the U.S. Treasury Market, the yields of bills are quoted in terms of equivalent bond yields (coupon yield equivalent). The equivalent bond yield is the coupon of a U.S. Treasury bond which, when trading at par, would give the same return as the bill. For a bill with less than or equal to 182 days to maturity the equivalent bond yield is the same as the money market yield except that it is quoted on the basis of a 365 day year. If Y_e is the equivalent bond yield then:

$$Y_e = \frac{100 \times R \times Ay}{(36000 - R \times D_{sm})} \qquad \text{if } D_{sm} = 182$$

7

where A_y is 365 days. However, if February 29th falls between the purchase date and the first anniversary of the purchase date, A_y is 366 days.

Example
For the U.S. Treasury Bill in the previous example there are 21 days to maturity, so:

$$Y_e = \frac{100 \times 7.0 \times 365}{(36000 - 7.0 \times 21)} = 7.126\%$$

For bills with more than 182 days to maturity the calculation of the equivalent bond yield is more complex, since the corresponding bond makes two coupon payments. Y_e is the coupon and yield which the bond must have such that an initial investment, P gives a return, F at maturity. The final return is made up of the following components:

a) The first coupon payment, which consists of the interest accrued by holding the bond for a fraction of a period:

$$P \times \left(\frac{D_{sm}}{365} - \frac{1}{2}\right) \times \frac{Y_e}{100}$$

b) Interest earned by reinvesting the first coupon payment at $Y_e\%$:

$$P \times \left(\frac{D_{sm}}{365} - \frac{1}{2}\right) \times \frac{Y_e}{100} \times \frac{Y_e}{200}$$

c) The final redemption payment:

$$P$$

d) The final coupon payment:

$$P \times \frac{Y_e}{200}$$

Equating the sum of these components to the face value gives the equation:

$$P + P \times \frac{Y_e}{200} + P \times \left(\frac{D_{sm}}{365} - \frac{1}{2}\right) \times \frac{Y_e}{100} \times \left(1 + \frac{Y_e}{200}\right) = F$$

which can be solved for Y_e. To summarise, the formulae for calculating the equivalent bond yield for a U.S. Treasury bill of any maturity are:

For bills with 182 days or less to maturity:

$$Y_e = \frac{100 \times R \times A_y}{(36000 - R \times D_{sm})}$$

For bills with more than 182 days to maturity:

$$Y_e = 200 \times \left(\frac{-v + \left(v^2 + (2 \times v - 1) \times \left(\frac{F}{P} - 1 \right) \right)^{\frac{1}{2}}}{2 \times v - 1} \right)$$

where:

$$v = \frac{D_{sm}}{A_y}$$

$$P = F \times \left(1 - \frac{R}{100} \times \frac{D_{sm}}{360} \right)$$

Y_e	= Equivalent bond yield %
R	= Rate of discount %
F	= Face value
A_y	= 365 days. However, if February 29th falls between the purchase date and the first anniversary of the purchase date Ay is 366 days.
D_{sm}	= Number of days from settlement to maturity

Example

A U.S. Treasury Bill maturing on 17th December, 1986 is purchased on 4th January, 1986 for $94.2167. There are 347 days between settlement and maturity. Therefore:

D_{sm}	= 347 days
A_y	= 365 days (February 29th not in year starting 4th January 1986)
P	= $94.2167
F	= $100
v	$= \dfrac{347}{365} = 0.9507$

and the equivalent bond yield, Y_e, is given by:

$$Y_e = 200 \times \left(\frac{-v + \left(v^2 + (2 \times v - 1) \times \left(\frac{100}{94.2167} - 1 \right) \right)^{\frac{1}{2}}}{2 \times v - 1} \right) = 6.36\%$$

Bills Sold before Maturity

If a bill is sold before maturity, the interest earned for the period for which it is held is given by:

$$I = \left(\frac{\left(1 - \frac{R_s}{100} \times \frac{D_{sm}}{A_d} \right)}{\left(1 - \frac{R_p}{100} \times \frac{D_{pm}}{A_d} \right)} - 1 \right) \times \frac{A_i}{(D_{pm} - D_{sm})} \times 100$$

where:

I = Simple interest earned for the period held %

R_p = Rate of discount at purchase %

R_s = Rate of discount at sale %

D_{pm} = Number of days from purchase to maturity

D_{sm} = Number of days from sale to maturity

A_d = Assumed number of days in a year for rate of discount

A_i = Assumed number of days in a year for interest earned

Example

A 147 day U.S. Treasury bill is bought at a rate of discount of 6.00%, held for 45 days and sold at a rate of discount of 5.85%. The interest earned calculated on the basis of a 365 day year is given by:

$$I = \left(\frac{\left(1 - \frac{5.85}{100} \times \frac{102}{360} \right)}{\left(1 - \frac{6.00}{100} \times \frac{147}{360} \right)} - 1 \right) \times \frac{365}{(147 - 102)} \times 100 = 6.59\%$$

Instruments Traded on a Yield Basis

The most important money market instruments which are traded on a yield basis are Certificates of Deposit (CDs).

Most CDs pay one coupon at maturity. However, some CDs make coupon payments before the maturity date.

CDs Paying One Coupon

At issue CDs are priced at par. At maturity the investor receives par plus a coupon payment. The coupon of a CD is expressed as an annual rate based on a 360 day or 365 day year depending on the market (the conventions are generally the same as for rates of discount). The value at maturity of a CD is given by the formula:

$$\text{Value at Maturity} = F \times \left(1 + \frac{G}{100} \times \frac{D_{im}}{A_y}\right)$$

where:
F = Face value of the CD
G = Coupon rate %
D_{im} = Number of days from the issue date to maturity
A_y = Assumed number of days in a year

At issue the yield of a CD is equal to its coupon. After issue the yield will change in response to movements in interest rates. To calculate the price of a CD for a given yield the formula is:

$$P = F \times \frac{\left(1 + \frac{G}{100} \times \frac{D_{im}}{A_y}\right)}{\left(1 + \frac{Y}{100} \times \frac{D_{sm}}{A_y}\right)}$$

where:
P = Price
F = Face value
G = Coupon rate %
Y = Yield %
D_{im} = Number of days from issue to maturity
D_{sm} = Number of days from settlement to maturity
A_y = Assumed number of days in a year

Example
An 8.0%, 180 day CD is sold 45 days before maturity on a yield of 7.75%. The yield and coupon are quoted on a 360 day basis. The value at maturity per $100 face value is:

$$100 \times \left(1 + \frac{8}{100} \times \frac{180}{360}\right) = \$104$$

The price is given by:

$$P = 100 \times \frac{\left(1 + \dfrac{8}{100} \times \dfrac{180}{360}\right)}{\left(1 + \dfrac{7.75}{100} \times \dfrac{45}{360}\right)} = \$103.0022$$

CDs Sold before Maturity If a CD is sold before maturity, the interest earned for the holding period is given by:

$$I = \left(\frac{\left(1 + \dfrac{Y_p}{100} \times \dfrac{D_{pm}}{A_y}\right)}{\left(1 + \dfrac{Y_s}{100} \times \dfrac{D_{sm}}{A_y}\right)} - 1\right) \times \frac{A_i}{(D_{pm} - D_{sm})} \times 100$$

where:

I = Simple interest earned over the holding period %

Y_p = Yield of the CD at purchase %

Y_s = Yield of the CD at sale %

D_{pm} = number of days between purchase and maturity

D_{sm} = number of days between sale and maturity

A_y = Assumed number of days in a year for CD yields

A_i = Assumed number of days in a year for interest earned

Example
An 8.0%, 180 day CD is sold at a yield of 8.0%, 45 days before maturity. Yields are quoted on the basis of a 360 day year. The interest earned based on a 360 day year is:

$$I = \left(\frac{\left(1 + \dfrac{8.0}{100} \times \dfrac{180}{360}\right)}{\left(1 + \dfrac{8.0}{100} \times \dfrac{45}{360}\right)} - 1\right) \times \frac{360}{(180 - 45)} \times 100 = 7.92\%$$

Note that although the CD is bought and sold on a yield of 8.0%, the simple interest earned over the holding period is not 8.0% but a lower figure, 7.92%.

CDs Paying More Than One Coupon

For CDs paying more than one coupon, the calculation of the price for a given yield is more complicated. First, it should be noted, that even if the CD pays a coupon at regular intervals, e.g. semi-annually, the coupon payments will not be exactly the same. The coupon payment per 100 face value at the end of a coupon period of D days is given by:

$$\text{Coupon payment} = \frac{D \times G}{A_y}$$

where G% is the coupon rate and A_y the assumed number of days in a year. Since the number of days in a coupon period can vary (between 181 to 184 for a semi-annual coupon), the coupon payments are not constant.

The principles behind the calculation of the price of a CD paying more than one coupon are best illustrated by a simple example. Suppose a CD has three coupon payments outstanding. The number of days in each coupon period are D_1, D_2 and D_3 and the corresponding cash flows CF_1, CF_2 and CF_3 (CF_3 includes the principal repayment as well as the coupon payment). The CD is purchased for settlement D_{sf} days before the first coupon.

settlement

First, the value of the cash flow CF_3 is calculated at the date of the second coupon payment, discounted at a yield of Y%. This value is:

$$\frac{CF_3}{\left(1 + \frac{Y}{100} \times \frac{D_3}{A_y}\right)} = FCF_2$$

since this is the amount that would have to be invested at the date of the second coupon at a yield of Y% to give a cash flow of CF_3 at maturity.

13

Thus, at the second coupon date a cash flow of CF_2 is received along with a series of future cash flows worth FCF_2. The value of these cash flows at the date of the first coupon is:

$$\frac{CF_2 + FCF_2}{\left(1 + \frac{Y}{100} \times \frac{D_2}{A_y}\right)} = FCF_1$$

At the first coupon date a cash flow of CF_1 is received along with a series of future cash flows worth FCF_1. The value of these cash flows at the settlement date is:

$$\frac{CF_1 + FCF_1}{\left(1 + \frac{Y}{100} \times \frac{D_{sf}}{A_y}\right)}$$

which is simply the price of the CD.

The calculation procedure can be summarised by the general formula:

$$P = \frac{F}{Z(N)} + \frac{G \times F}{100 \times A_y} \times \sum_{i=1}^{N} \frac{D_i}{Z(i)}$$

where:

$$Z(1) = \left(1 + \frac{D_{sf}}{A_y} \times \frac{Y}{100}\right)$$

$$Z(i) = Z(i-1) \times \left(1 + \frac{D_i}{A_y} \times \frac{Y}{100}\right) \qquad \text{for } i = 2,..,N$$

N	= Number of coupon payments outstanding
P	= Price of the CD
F	= Face value
Y	= Yield %
D_i	= Number of days in the ith coupon period
D_{sf}	= Number of days from settlement to the first coupon
G	= Coupon rate %
A_y	= Assumed number of days in a year

Example

An 8% semi-annual U.S. $ CD is traded for settlement on the 24th August, 1986 on a yield of 7.75%. Suppose there are three coupon payments remaining on 8th October, 1986; 8th April, 1987 and 8th October, 1987. The market convention is a 360 day year. What is the price per $100 face value?

N = 3 (there are three coupon payments outstanding)

D_1 = 183 (the number of days between the previous coupon on 8th April, 1986 and the first coupon on 8th October, 1986)

D_2 = 182 (the number of days between the first coupon on 8th October, 1986 and the second coupon on 8th April, 1987)

D_3 = 183 (the number of days between the second coupon on 8th April, 1987 and 8th October, 1987)

D_{sf} = 45 (the number of days between settlement on 24th August, 1986 and the first coupon on 8th October, 1986)

Y = 7.75%
G = 8%
A_y = 360
F = $100

$$Z(1) = \left(1 + \frac{45}{360} \times \frac{7.75}{100}\right) = 1.00969$$

$$Z(2) = 1.00969 \times \left(1 + \frac{182}{360} \times \frac{7.75}{100}\right) = 1.04925$$

$$Z(3) = 1.04925 \times \left(1 + \frac{183}{360} \times \frac{7.75}{100}\right) = 1.09058$$

Therefore, the price is given by:

$$P = \frac{100}{1.09058} + \frac{8 \times 100}{100 \times 360} \times \left(\frac{183}{1.00969} + \frac{182}{1.04925} + \frac{183}{1.09058}\right)$$

$$= \$103.3052$$

IV Yields of Bonds

Bonds are usually traded on the basis of price. The price that is usually quoted is the clean or flat price. The total price that must be paid for a bond is the dirty price, which is also known as the gross or full price. The dirty price is equal to the clean price plus the accrued interest. The accrued interest, which is usually positive, compensates the seller for the fact that he has held the bond for part of a coupon period, but is forgoing the whole of the next coupon (see 'Accrued Interest Calculations', page 79). When the bond pays a coupon, the dirty price will drop by the coupon payment, but the clean price will not change. It is for this reason that clean prices are usually quoted.

Bonds have more complicated cash flow patterns than money market instruments, which usually make only a single payment at maturity. A straight bond pays a fixed coupon at regular intervals up to and including the maturity date when it is redeemed at face value. However, the cash flow patterns can be more complicated than this. For example, stepped coupon bonds pay a coupon which changes according to a schedule determined at issue. Other bond issues are not redeemed on one date but over a period of time by means of a sinking fund.*

The wide variation of cash flow patterns for bonds means that price cannot be used for comparing the relative attractiveness of bonds. The usual starting point for valuing a bond is to calculate the yield. There are three types of yield that are commonly used:

a) Current Yield
b) Simple Yield-to-Maturity
c) Yield-to-Maturity (Redemption Yield)

---

*For details of the wide variety of structures that have been used in the international bond markets see 'Innovations in the Structures of International Securities', CSFB Research, 1986.

These differ in their sophistication in taking into account the relative value of payments received at different times. Of the three, yield-to-maturity is both the most sophisticated and the most commonly used.

Usually, bonds are redeemed at face value. In the descriptions of bond yields below, this has been assumed to be the case. Furthermore, following the normal convention, prices are quoted per 100 units face value.

A minor modification suffices to cope with bonds redeemed at values other than par; the coupon and price of the bond are scaled accordingly. For example, in the calculation of yield, a 6% bond priced at 100 and redeemed at 102 is equivalent to a bond priced at:

$$\frac{100}{1.02} = 98.04$$

and paying a coupon of:

$$\frac{6}{1.02} = 5.88\%$$

Current Yield

Current yield is the simplest measure of yield. It is also known as flat yield, interest yield, income yield, or running yield. Current yield is the income received per annum for an investment equal to the face value and is given by the formula:

$$CY = \frac{G}{P_c} \times 100$$

where:
CY = Current yield %
G = Coupon rate %
P_c = Clean price, i.e. excluding accrued interest

Example
An 8% coupon bond has a clean price of $96. The current yield is:

$$CY = \frac{8}{96} \times 100 = 8.33\%$$

Although current yield is easy to calculate, it is a very crude measure of the value of a security. It does not account for the effects of any capital appreciation or depreciation. For example, if the 8% coupon bond pays annually, then, if bought at the start of the final coupon period and held to maturity, i.e. for one year, the return is:

$$\left(\frac{100 + 8 - 96}{96}\right) \times 100 = 12.5\%$$

which is well above the current yield. Current yield is a sensible measure of value only when the term to maturity is long, since capital gain/loss effects are then small.

The use of the clean price in the calculation of current yield is not particularly logical. After all, if a bond is bought part of the way through a coupon period, then the return produced by that bond should be calculated with respect to price actually paid for the bond, i.e. the dirty price.

Simple Yield-to-Maturity

Simple yield-to-maturity, which is commonly used in the Japanese market, tries to take into account the effect of the maturity on the value of a bond to the investor. Any capital gain or loss on the bond is deemed to occur uniformly over its life. Simple yield-to-maturity is given by the formula:

$$SY = \frac{G + \dfrac{100 - P_c}{M_y}}{P_c} \times 100$$

where:
SY = Simple yield-to-maturity %
G = Coupon rate %
M_y = Maturity in years
P_c = Clean price

Example
An 8% annual coupon, 5 year bond is priced at $96. The simple yield-to-maturity is:

$$SY = \frac{8 + \dfrac{100 - 96}{5}}{96} \times 100 = 9.17\%$$

If the maturity of the bond were 10 years the simple yield would be 8.75%. This is lower than the simple yield for the 5 year bond reflecting the fact that the capital amortisation occurs over a longer period.

The chief problem with simple yield-to-maturity is that it does not allow for compounding interest. For example, suppose an investor purchases a two year zero coupon bond for $90. Its simple yield-to-maturity is:

$$SY = \frac{0 + \dfrac{100 - 90}{2}}{90} \times 100 = 5.56\%$$

However, if the investor put $90 on deposit for two years at 5.56% he would earn more than $100, since the interest earned after one year can be reinvested. In fact he would receive:

$$90 \times \left(1 + \frac{5.56}{100}\right)^2 = \$100.28$$

Yield-to-maturity, which is described in the next section, takes into account the effect of compounding interest.

Yield-to-Maturity (Redemption Yield)

Yield-to-maturity is the most commonly used measure of the value of a bond. It is also called redemption yield, or often just yield. It makes allowance for the relative values of payments received at different times.

The concept of present value is central to the understanding of how yield-to-maturity is calculated. $1 received now is worth $1, but how much is $1 received one year from now worth? If it is possible to invest at an annual rate of interest of I% then

$$\frac{\$1}{\left(1 + \dfrac{I}{100}\right)}$$

invested now will give $1 in one year. This is the present value of a future cash flow of $1 received in one year's time. How much is $1 received in two years' time worth? If it is possible to invest at an annual rate of interest of I% for two successive years then, allowing for compounding of interest,

$$\frac{\$1}{\left(1 + \dfrac{I}{100}\right)^2}$$

invested now will give $1 in two years. This is the present value of a future cash flow of $1 received in two years' time. In general, the present value of $1 received in N year's time is:

$$\frac{\$1}{\left(1 + \dfrac{I}{100}\right)^N}$$

if it is assumed that it is possible to invest at an annual rate of I% throughout the period.

The present value of a cash flow decreases the further in the future it is received. It also decreases the higher the rate at which it is possible to invest. The graph shows the present value of $1 received at different times and for different investment rates.

Present Value of a Future Cash Flow of $1

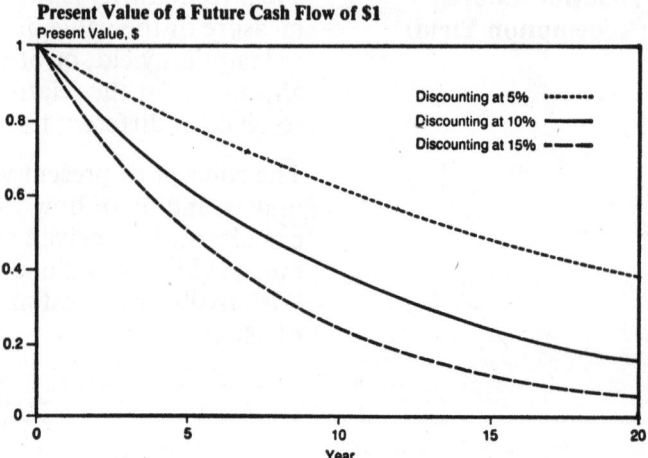

Present Value, $

Discounting at 5% ·······
Discounting at 10% ———
Discounting at 15% — — —

Year

When talking about the present values of cash flows the investment rate, I, is generally called the discount rate. Calculating the present value is termed discounting the cash flow.

The idea behind the calculation of yield-to-maturity is that the value of a bond is equal to the sum of the present values of all its future cash flows. The yield-to-maturity is the discount rate which causes the sum of present values to equal the total price paid for the bond, including accrued interest. All present values are calculated using the same discount rate.

Example
Consider a 10% annual coupon bond with 5 years to maturity. Suppose its yield-to-maturity is 8%. What is its price?

After one year there is a payment of $10. The present value of this cash flow discounted at a rate of 8% is:

$$\frac{\$10}{\left(1 + \frac{8}{100}\right)} = \$9.26$$

After two years there is again a payment of $8. The present value of this cash flow discounted at the same rate of 8% is:

$$\frac{\$10}{\left(1 + \frac{8}{100}\right)^2} = \$8.57$$

Proceeding in this way the present values of all the cash flows generated by the bond can be calculated. These are shown in the table below.

Year	Cash Flow	Discount Factor	Present Value
1	10	0.926	9.26
2	10	0.857	8.57
3	10	0.794	7.94
4	10	0.735	7.35
5	110	0.681	74.86
			107.99

The sum of the present values of the future cash flows is $107.99, the dirty price of the bond.

How does the price of a bond change as its yield changes? Increasing the yield causes the present values of all the cash flows to fall so their sum, which is the price of the bond, decreases. Conversely, if the yield decreases, the price increases. The graph shows a plot of price against yield for a 10% annual coupon, 5 year bond.

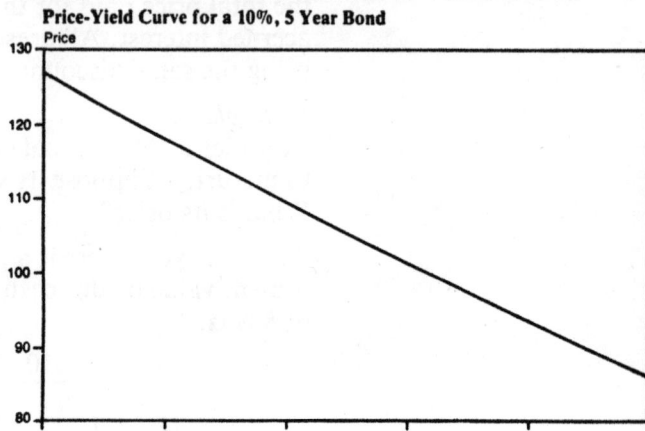

Price-Yield Curve for a 10%, 5 Year Bond

For a bond paying an annual coupon which is priced at par, the yield is equal to the coupon rate. (Actually, this is not exactly correct. See page 90.)

Expressed mathematically, the relationship between the price, P, and the yield-to-maturity, Y%, for a bond paying an annual coupon of G% is, on a coupon date:

$$P = \sum_{i=1}^{M_y} \frac{G}{\left(1 + \dfrac{Y}{100}\right)^i} + \frac{100}{\left(1 + \dfrac{Y}{100}\right)^{M_y}}$$

where M_y is the number of years to maturity. This formula needs to be modified for bonds which pay interest semi-annually and for the case when there is a non-integral number of coupon periods remaining. See 'Fractional Coupon Periods', page 30 and 'Semi-Annual and Quarterly Coupons', page 27 for details.

Of course, in practice it is usually the price of the bond that is known and one wants to calculate the yield-to-maturity. The way that this can be done is described in Appendix A. Since the calculation is tedious to do by hand, it is best left to a computer or a programmable calculator.

If the yield-to-maturity remains constant, how does the price of a bond vary as it approaches maturity? For the 10% coupon, 5 year bond its price was $107.99 to yield 8%. As the bond approaches the maturity date its clean price will decrease towards par. After one year the price of the bond can be calculated as shown below:

Year	Cash Flow	Discount Factor	Present Value
1	10	0.926	9.26
2	10	0.857	8.57
3	10	0.794	7.94
4	110	0.735	80.85
			106.62

Thus the price of the bond after one year has decreased to $106.62. Suppose the bond is sold after one year, what would be the return? One coupon payment of $10 is received but a capital loss of $107.99 − $106.62 = $1.37 is incurred. Therefore the return over the year is:

$$\frac{(10 - 1.37) \times 100}{107.99} = 8\%$$

which is simply the yield-to-maturity.

The graph shows a plot of clean price against time to maturity for three 5 year bonds with 6%, 8% and 10% coupons at a constant yield of 8%.

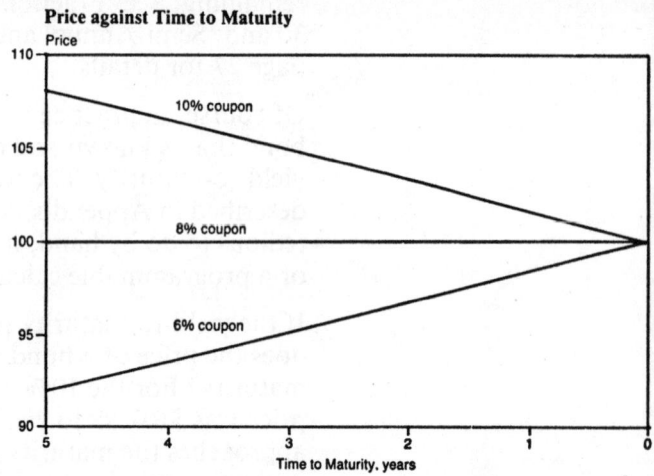

Price against Time to Maturity

Of course, in practice, the clean price of a bond trading above or below par does not move smoothly towards par at maturity since yields do not remain constant. However, there will always be a general drift towards par at maturity. This is illustrated by the graph below, which shows a plot of clean price against date for two U.K. gilt-edged securities close to maturity.

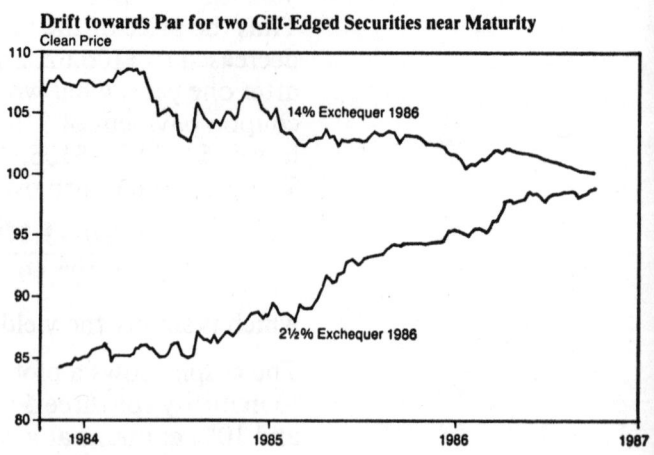

Drift towards Par for two Gilt-Edged Securities near Maturity

Coupon Reinvestment

Suppose an investor buys a bond at a yield of 8% and holds it until maturity. He will only realise a return of 8% if he can reinvest all coupon payments received before maturity also at 8%. If the reinvestment rate is greater/less than 8% then his realised return will be greater/less than the yield-to-maturity of 8%. This uncertainty in the return that will actually be obtained over the life of the bond is termed reinvestment risk.

It is possible to calculate the realised return on a bond under various assumptions about the rates at which coupon income can be reinvested. The simplest form of analysis is to assume that all coupons are reinvested at the same rate.

Example
A 10% annual coupon, 5 year bond, priced at $107.98 has a yield-to-maturity of 8%. Suppose the reinvestment rate is 7%. The table shows the cash flows received in each year and their value if reinvested at 7% until maturity.

Year	Cash Flow	Value at Year 5 at 7% Reinvestment Rate
1	10	13.11
2	10	12.25
3	10	11.45
4	10	10.70
5	110	110.00
		157.51

At maturity, the investor receives a total of $157.51. This corresponds to an annual rate of return on his original investment of:

$$\left(\left(\frac{157.51}{107.99}\right)^{1/5} - 1\right) \times 100 = 7.84\%$$

which is less than the yield-to-maturity of 8%. The graph shows the realised return at various reinvestment rates for 5 year bonds with 6%, 8% and 10% coupons all yielding 8%.

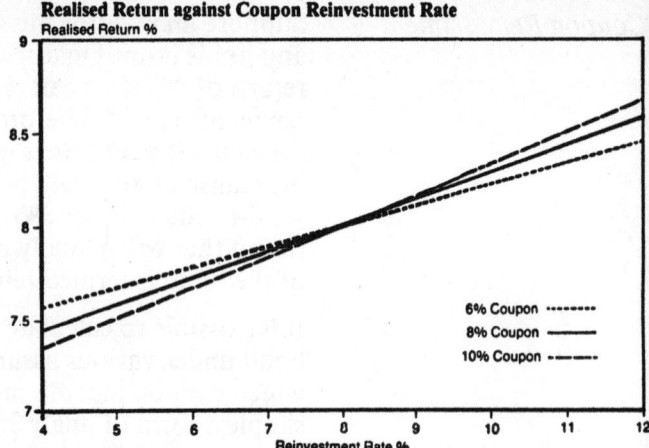

Realised Return against Coupon Reinvestment Rate

Only for a reinvestment rate of 8% does the investor realise a return equal to the yield-to-maturity.

The return produced by a bond can be divided into three components:

— redemption proceeds;
— coupon income;
— interest earned by reinvesting coupon income.

The graph shows the proportion of return produced by each of the components as a function of coupon for a yield of 8% and a reinvestment rate of 8%.

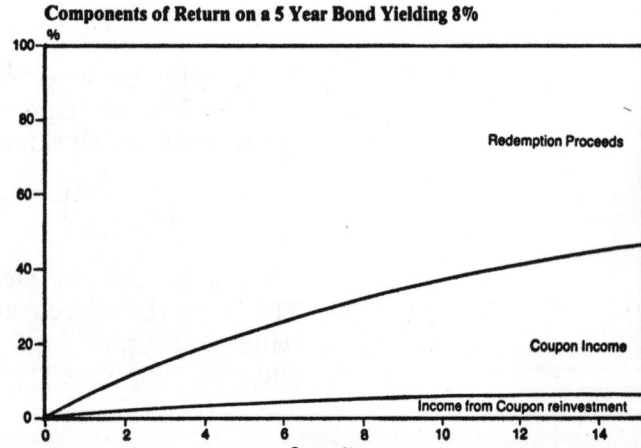

Components of Return on a 5 Year Bond Yielding 8%

As the coupon increases, a higher proportion of the total return comes from coupon income and interest on coupon income. Thus the realised return on bonds with high coupons tends to be more sensitive to the reinvestment rate.

Yield-to-Maturity, Current Yield and Simple Yield-to-Maturity

The yield-to-maturity, current-yield and simple yield-to-maturity are the same only for bonds priced at par. For bonds not at par, the following inequalities hold when there is more than one coupon payment outstanding:

Above par:
Current yield > Yield-to-maturity > Simple Yield-to-maturity

Below par:
Current yield < Yield-to-maturity < Simple Yield-to-maturity

The graph shows a plot of yield-to-maturity, current yield and simple yield-to-maturity against price for an 8% annual coupon, 5 year bond.

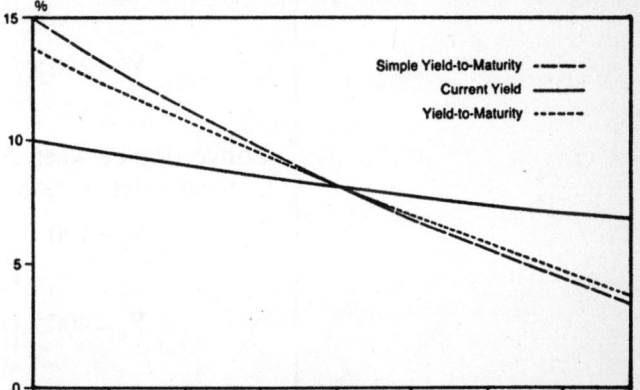

Yield-to-Maturity, Current Yield & Simple Yield-to-Maturity against Price

Semi-Annual and Quarterly Coupons

For a bond which pays a coupon H times per annum, there are two commonly used ways of discounting its cash flows when calculating its yield-to-maturity. Cash flows are either discounted on an annual basis or on the basis of a coupon period. When discounting on an annual basis, $1 received in N coupon periods time has the present value of:

27

$$\frac{\$1}{\left(1 + \dfrac{Y_a}{100}\right)^{N/H}}$$

where Y_a is called the annually compounded yield. When discounting on the basis of a coupon period, $1 received in N coupon periods time has the present value of:

$$\frac{\$1}{\left(1 + \dfrac{Y_h}{100 \times H}\right)^{N}}$$

where Y_h is the semi-annually (H = 2) or quarterly compounded (H = 4) yield. Equating the present values gives the formulae:

Converting between Annually and Semi-annually Compounded Yields:

$$Y_a = 100 \times \left[\left(1 + \frac{Y_s}{200}\right)^{2} - 1\right]$$

$$Y_s = 200 \times \left[\left(1 + \frac{Y_a}{100}\right)^{1/2} - 1\right]$$

Converting between Annually and Quarterly Compounded Yields:

$$Y_a = 100 \times \left[\left(1 + \frac{Y_q}{400}\right)^{4} - 1\right]$$

$$Y_q = 400 \times \left[\left(1 + \frac{Y_a}{100}\right)^{1/4} - 1\right]$$

where:
Y_a = Annually compounded yield %
Y_s = Semi-annually compounded yield %
Y_q = Quarterly compounded yield %

Example
A bond has a semi-annually compounded yield of 10%. The annually compounded yield is:

$$100 \times \left[\left(1 + \frac{10}{200}\right)^{2} - 1\right] = 10.25\%$$

If the annually compounded yield is 8%, then the semi-annually compounded yield is:

$$200 \times \left[\left(1 + \frac{8}{100}\right)^{1/2} - 1 \right] = 7.85\%$$

The annually compounded yield is always greater then the semi-annually compounded yield, the difference increasing as yields rise:

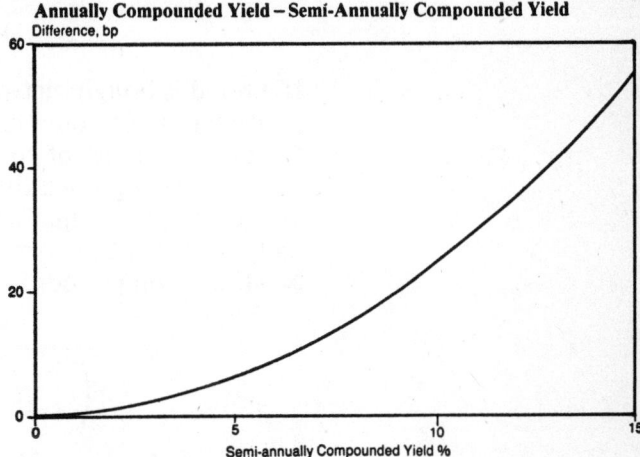

Annually Compounded Yield – Semi-Annually Compounded Yield
Difference, bp

Semi-annually Compounded Yield %

Clearly, it is important to know on what basis a yield is quoted. Typically, in a market that is dominated by semi-annual coupon bonds (e.g. gilt-edged or U.S. Treasury market) semi-annually compounded yields are quoted. If annual coupon bonds predominate (e.g. Euromarkets) annually compounded yields are quoted. The reason for this practice is that on a coupon date a semi-annual bond priced at par has a semi-annually compounded yield equal to its coupon. On a coupon date an annual coupon bond priced at par has an annually compounded yield equal to its coupon.

For the rarer case of bonds paying a quarterly coupon, yields are usually quoted on a semi-annually or annually compounded basis, depending on the market in which they occur.

Fractional Coupon
Periods

So far, it has been assumed that there is a whole number of coupon periods remaining. In such a case it is obvious how each future cash flow should be discounted. If the bond pays H coupons per annum and the yield compounded H times per annum is $Y_h\%$, then $1 received after N coupon periods has a present value of:

$$\frac{\$1}{\left(1 + \dfrac{Y_h}{H \times 100}\right)^N}$$

If a bond is bought between coupon dates, it is neccessary to discount cash flows received a fractional number of coupon periods in the future. The approach that is usually taken is to assume, in effect, that interest is compounded daily so that the present value of $1 received after $N + K$ coupon periods is:

$$\frac{\$1}{\left(1 + \dfrac{Y_h}{H \times 100}\right)^{N+K}}$$

where N is the number of whole periods and K is the fraction of a period left over. (Occasionally, simple interest is used to discount fractional periods. See Appendix D.)

Example
An 8% annual coupon bond has a yield of 8% and 4½ years to maturity. After ½ year there is a payment of $8, which has a present value of:

$$\frac{\$8}{\left(1 + \dfrac{8}{100}\right)^{1/2}} = \$7.70$$

After 1½ years there is again a payment of $8, which has a present value of:

$$\frac{\$8}{\left(1 + \dfrac{8}{100}\right)^{1+1/2}} = \$7.13$$

Proceeding in this way, the dirty price of the bond is found to be $103.93:

Year	Cash Flow	Discount Factor	Present Value
0.5	8	0.962	7.70
1.5	8	0.891	7.13
2.5	8	0.825	6.60
3.5	8	0.764	6.11
4.5	108	0.707	76.39
			103.93

The clean price of the bond is found by subtracting half a year's accrued interest, which gives $99.93. (This is not exactly equal to par due to the fact that accrued interest is calculated on a simple interest basis whilst daily compounding is assumed when discounting payments received after fractional periods. See page 90.)

One of the major differences between markets in the method for calculating quoted yields lies in the way in which the fraction of a period to the next payment, K, is calculated. Generally the same method is used as for accrued interest calculations (see page 88).

Assuming equal length coupon periods, the dirty price of a bond paying a constant coupon is related to the yield by the formula:

$$P_d = V^K \times \left(\frac{G}{H} \times \frac{(1 - V^N)}{(1 - V)} + 100 \times V^{N-1} \right)$$

where:

$$V = \frac{1}{\left(1 + \dfrac{Y_h}{H \times 100} \right)}$$

P_d = Dirty price
Y_h = Yield compounded H times per annum %
G = Coupon rate %
H = Coupon frequency
N = Number of coupon payments outstanding
K = Fraction of a period from settlement to the next coupon payment calculated according to the appropriate market convention.

Appendix B gives a more general version of this formula and shows how the yield can be calculated for a given price.

For a perpetual bond the number of outstanding payments, N, is infinite and the above formula simplifies to:

$$P_d = \frac{V^K}{(1-V)} \times \frac{G}{H}$$

At a coupon date $K = 1$ and P_d is the same as the clean price, P_c. The yield is then given by:

$$Y_h = \frac{G}{P_c} \times 100$$

i.e. the yield of a perpetual bond on a coupon date is equal to the current yield.

A Bond in its Final Coupon Period

A bond in its final coupon period is, in terms of its cash flows, directly comparable to a money market instrument. For this reason, simple interest yield calculations are sometimes used. This, for example, is the case in the U.S. market.

Using a simple interest approach, the yield for a bond in its final coupon period is related to the dirty price by the formula:

$$Y = \frac{\left(100 + \dfrac{G}{H} - P_d\right)}{P_d} \times \frac{A_y}{D_{sm}} \times 100$$

where:
Y = Simple interest yield, %
P_d = Dirty price
G = Coupon rate %
D_{sm} = Number of days from settlement to maturity (actual days or days calculated on the basis of a 30 day month)
A_y = Assumed number of days in a year
H = Coupon frequency

Quoted yields for U.S. Treasuries take A_y as twice the number of days in a coupon period and D_{sm} as the actual number of days from settlement to maturity.

Quoted yields for U.S. Federal Agencies take A_y as 360 days and D_{sm} as the number of days from settlement to maturity based on a year of twelve 30 day months (see page 81).

Example
A 9% U.S. Treasury bond is bought for settlement on 1st May, 1986 at a dirty price of $102.71 with maturity date 1st August, 1986. The previous coupon was on 1st February, 1986, so the number of days in the final coupon period is 181, and $A_y = 2 \times 181 = 362$ days. The actual number of days from settlement to maturity is 92. Therefore:

$$Y = \frac{\left(100 + \dfrac{9}{2} - 102.71\right)}{102.71} \times \frac{362}{92} \times 100 = 6.857\%$$

A U.S. Federal Agency with identical cash flows to the U.S. Treasury has $A_y = 360$ and $D_{sm} = 90$. Therefore the yield is:

$$Y = \frac{\left(100 + \dfrac{9}{2} - 102.71\right)}{102.71} \times \frac{360}{90} \times 100 = 6.971\%$$

A Certificate of Deposit with identical cash flows to the U.S. Treasury has $A_y = 360$, $D_{sm} = 92$ giving a quoted yield of 6.820%.

Finally, the same method which is generally used to calculate the yields for U.S. Treasuries with more than one coupon period to maturity can equally well be applied to a bond in its final coupon period. This, in effect, assumes daily compounding of interest when discounting a fraction of a coupon period (see "Fractional Coupon Periods", page 30). The semi-annually compounded yield is found to be 6.915%.

As the example shows, for a given set of cash flows, more than one yield may be quoted in different markets. The methods described above for calculating yields of securities making one single payment are all widely used. Therefore, the moral is that, when comparing the relative attractiveness of different securities, it is important to ensure that their yields have been computed on the same basis.

Money Market Yields for Bonds paying more than one Coupon

It is common for an investor to want to compare the yield on a bond with the yield of a money market instrument of similar maturity. For example, the purchase of a bond might be funded by issuing a CD.

For a bond in its final coupon period the money market yield can be calculated using simple interest (see page 32).

For a bond with more than one coupon payment outstanding, the money market yield can be calculated in an analogous fashion to a CD with the same cash flows (see page 13). The only difference is that, in contrast to a CD, a bond normally makes constant coupon payments irrespective of the precise number of days in a coupon period. The dirty price is related to the money market yield by the formula:

$$P_d = \frac{100}{Z(N)} + \frac{G}{H} \times \sum_{i=1}^{N} \frac{1}{Z(i)}$$

where:

$$Z(1) = (1 + \frac{D_{sf}}{A_y} \times \frac{Y_m}{100})$$

$$Z(i) = Z(i-1) \times (1 + \frac{D_i}{A_y} \times \frac{Y_m}{100}) \quad \text{for } i = 2,..,N$$

N = Number of coupon payments outstanding

P_d = Dirty price

Y_m = Money market yield %

D_i = Number of days between the $i\text{-}1$th and ith coupon payment

D_{sf} = Number of days from settlement to the first coupon

G = Coupon rate %

A_y = Assumed number of days in a year for money market instruments

H = Coupon frequency

It is convenient to make the approximation that the number of days in a coupon period is constant, i.e. to assume that:

$$D_i = \frac{365}{H}$$

Making this approximation, the formula simplifies to give:

$$P_d = \frac{1}{\left(1 + \frac{D_{sf}}{A_y} \times \frac{Y_m}{100}\right)} \times \left(\frac{G}{H} \times \frac{(1 - V_m^N)}{(1 - V_m)} + 100 \times V_m^{N-1}\right)$$

where:

$$V_m = \frac{1}{\left(1 + \frac{365}{A_y \times H} \times \frac{Y_m}{100}\right)}$$

N = Number of coupon payments outstanding

P_d = Dirty price

Y_m = Money market yield %

D_{sf} = Number of days from settlement to the first coupon

G = Coupon rate %

A_y = Assumed number of days in a year for money market instruments

H = Coupon frequency

On coupon dates this formula is identical to that for the bond yield given on page 31 with:

$$Y_m = \frac{A_y}{360} \times Y_h$$

where Y_h is the bond yield compounded H times per annum. Thus, for example, if the money market assumes 360 days in a year and the bond yield is 8%, then at a coupon date the money market yield is:

$$Y_m = \frac{360 \times 8}{365} = 7.89\%$$

Between coupon periods the money market yield differs from this value, since the money market yield formula discounts the first fractional period, using simple interest, by the factor:

$$\frac{1}{\left(1 + D_{sf} \times \frac{Y_m}{A_y} \frac{}{100}\right)}$$

whilst the bond yield formula uses compound interest, discounting by the factor:

$$\frac{1}{\left(1 + \frac{Y_h}{100 \times H}\right)^K}$$

where K is the fraction of a period to the next coupon payment and is given approximately by:

$$K = \frac{D_{sf} \times H}{365}$$

The graph below shows a plot of the money market yield of an 8% coupon bond with a bond yield of 8% against maturity. The money market basis is a year of 360 days.

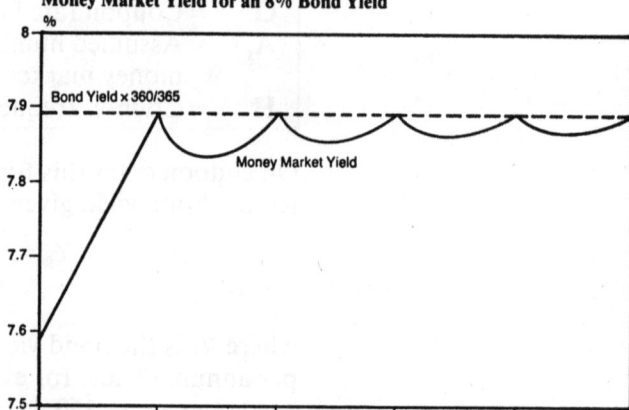

Money Market Yield for an 8% Bond Yield

36

Effect of Allowing
for Precise Payment Dates

The basic method for calculating yield-to-maturity which is described above is the one most commonly used. It can be criticised on the grounds that it assumes that all coupon periods are of equal length. This might not be the case for mundane reasons like the fact that not all years have 365 days. However, it can happen (or has been arranged to happen!) that a scheduled payment falls due on a non-business day, so the actual payment takes place on the next business day. Any delays in payment have the effect of reducing the yield.

The reduction in yield tends to be largest when it is the redemption payment that is delayed and when the bond has a short term to maturity. To illustrate this effect, consider an 8% annual coupon bond trading at par. Suppose the final payment of interest and capital is delayed by two days (this would usually be the case if the scheduled payment date were a Saturday). The graph shows the drop in yield in basis points caused by this shift for various maturities.

Fall in Yield caused by a two day deferment in the Redemption Payment

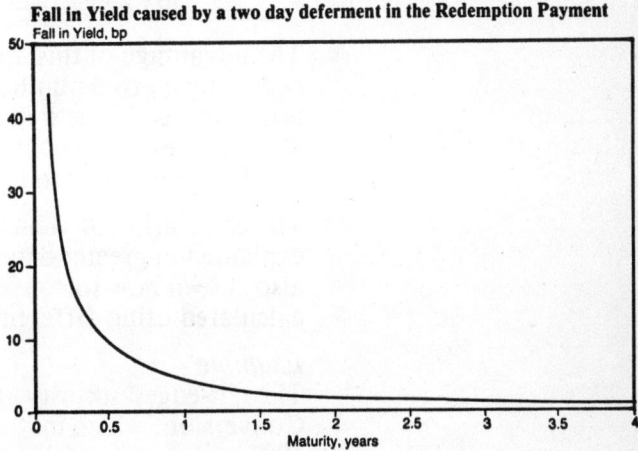

It can be seen that for bonds with a maturity of less than one year the drop in yield can be significant.

To obtain a more consistent yield figure, it is necessary to calculate the precise number of calendar days from settlement to each cash flow. Any given cash flow is discounted by a discount factor raised to the power of the number of days from settlement to that cash flow. The sum of cash flows discounted in this fashion is then equated to the dirty price. The general formula is:

$$P_d = \sum_i \frac{CF_i}{\left(1 + \frac{Y_h}{H \times 100}\right)^{\frac{D_i \times H}{A_y}}}$$

where:

P_d = Dirty price
CF_i = The ith cash flow
D_i = Number of calendar days from settlement to the ith cash flow, making allowance for weekends and public holidays causing payment to be postponed
H = Yield compounding frequency
Y_h = Yield compounded H times per annum %
A_y = Number of days in a year (360, 365 or 365.25 according to choice)

The advantage of this approach is that a cash flow occurring a given number of days from settlement is discounted in the same fashion for any bond. This enables direct comparisons of yield figures for different bonds to be made.

The calculation of yields using this method is explained in greater detail in Appendix A. It is also shown how to convert between yields calculated using different choices for A_y and H.

Example
The gilt-edged security 10.25% Treasury Conversion, which matures on 10th February, 1987 and pays a semi-annual coupon, is traded for settlement on 2nd July, 1986 at a dirty price of £104.425. What is the semi-annually compounded yield based on a 365 day year?

The nominal payment date of the first coupon payment of £5.125 is 10th August, 1986. However, this date is in fact a Sunday, so payment will actually take place on 11th August, 1986, 40 days from settlement. Therefore, the discounted cash flow is:

$$£5.125 \times \left(1 + \frac{Y_h}{200}\right)^{-40/182.5}$$

The final coupon plus redemption payment of £105.125 is received on 10th February, 1987 (a Tuesday) which is 223 days from settlement. The discounted value of this cash flow is:

$$£105.125 \times \left(1 + \frac{Y_h}{200}\right)^{-223/182.5}$$

The two discounted cash flows must sum to the dirty price giving the equation:

$$104.425 = 5.125 \times \left(1 + \frac{Y_h}{200}\right)^{-40/182.5} + 105.125 \times \left(1 + \frac{Y_h}{200}\right)^{-223/182.5}$$

The value of Y_h which satisfies this equation is 9.462%.

Quoted yields often do not calculate the precise dates on which coupon payments fall, but just assume equal length coupon periods. The Consortium yields, which are quoted in the gilt-edged market, make such an approximation. The Consortium yield for the 10.25% Treasury Conversion 87 on the same settlement date was 9.529%, about 7 basis points above the more precisely calculated yield.

Net Yield

So far we have ignored any tax payments on the income received from a bond; the yields calculated have been gross yields. Net yield is calculated in a similar way to gross yield except that all the cash flows are net of tax.

The details of how the cash flows from a bond are taxed vary from country to country. For example, capital gains tax may be payable on any capital gain, taking the purchase price as either the clean price or the dirty price. Income tax is usually paid on coupon income. However, it might be the case that only the portion of the first coupon payment representing the interest accrued since purchase is liable for income tax. There are usually special tax regulations for low coupon bonds.

The actual levels of taxation depend on the specific investor. It is common to quote net yields for what is deemed to be a typical investor in the market.

Example
Currently, in the U.S. market net yields are quoted assuming a corporate tax rate of 46%. Furthermore, for a bond trading below par and with more than 12 months to maturity any capital gain is taxed at the corporate capital gains tax rate of 28%. Capital gains tax is paid on the difference between the clean price and the redemption payment.

Suppose a 6% annual coupon, 5 year U.S. Treasury bond is purchased for \$92.01 to yield 8%. The gross and net cash flows are shown in the table below.

Year	Gross CF	Net CF	PV Net CF at 4.66%
1	6.00	3.24	3.10
2	6.00	3.24	2.96
3	6.00	3.24	2.83
4	6.00	3.24	2.70
5	106.00	3.24+97.76	80.43
			92.01

There is a capital gain of $100 - 92.01 = \$7.99$. After paying capital gains tax at 28%, the redemption payment is effectively reduced to $100 - 7.99 \times 0.28 = \$97.76$. The net yield is found to be 4.66%.

It is common to estimate the net yield of a discount bond using the following approximation. The yield-to-maturity is split into two components, coupon interest and capital gain. If Y is the yield then the coupon rate G is taken to represent income whilst the remainder, $Y - G$, represents capital gain. If X_i and X_c are the rates of income tax and capital gains tax respectively then the net yield, Y_n, is given approximately by:

$$Y_n = G \times (1 - X_i) + (Y - G) \times (1 - X_c)$$

For the example this gives an estimate of the net yield:

$$Y_n = 6 \times (1 - 0.46) + (8 - 6) \times (1 - 0.28) = 4.68\%$$

which is quite close to the precisely calculated value of 4.66%.

Net yield is a better measure of the value of a bond to taxed individuals than gross yield and it can sometimes be a better indicator of the way a bond trades. For example, suppose there is a sizeable body of investors who pay a lower rate of capital gains tax than income tax. For these investors a low coupon bond, where a large part of the return is capital gain, might be an attractive investment even though its gross yield is lower than a similar high coupon bond. The net yields of the two bonds might be closer.

The above calculation of net yield assumes that tax is deducted at the same time as payment. It is usually possible to defer tax payments — this has the effect of increasing the net yield. The graph shows for the bond in the above example the gain in net yield which can be achieved if all tax payments can be deferred by the same amount.

Gain in Yield by Deferring Tax Payments

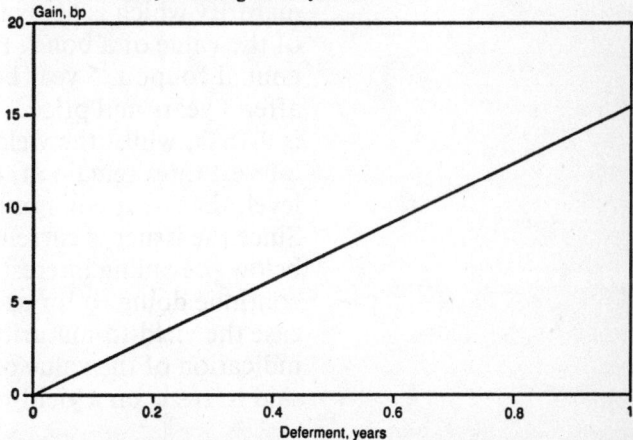

41

If all payments can be deferred by one year there is a gain in net yield of 15 bp. For higher tax rates the gain would be even greater.

Yield-to-Call and
Yield-to-Put

For bonds with call or put options the yield-to-maturity can still be calculated on the assumption that the option is not exercised and the bond held to maturity. However, the yield-to-maturity might mislead the investor as to the value of the bond.

For example, consider a 10% annual coupon bond with 5 years to maturity, priced at $107.99 to yield 8%. Suppose the issuer has the option to redeem it at par on the coupon date in three years time. If the call option is exercised, then the yield can be calculated as for a 3 year bond. This yield is termed the yield-to-call. For the example it is 6.96%, below the yield-to-maturity of 8%.

Since the bond was issued at a price of $100, interest rates have fallen. If interest rates remain at, or below, the current level, then the issuer will probably call the bond. The reason for this is that he is currently borrowing at a rate above prevailing interest rates so he will want to refinance his borrowing at the earliest possible opportunity. Thus, for this example, it is the yield-to-call which is likely to give a better indication of the value of the bond. The bond is said to trade on a yield-to-call basis.

For a bond trading below par it is the yield-to-maturity which is likely to give a better indication of the value of a bond. For example, for a 6% annual coupon, 5 year bond with a call option after 3 years and priced at $92.01 the yield-to-call is 9.16%, whilst the yield-to-maturity is 8%. If interest rates remain at, or above, the current level, the issuer will not exercise the call option. Since the issuer is currently borrowing at a rate below prevailing interest rates, he will try to continue doing so for as long as possible. In this case the yield-to-maturity is likely to give a better indication of the value of the bond. The bond is said to trade on a yield-to-maturity basis.

The yield on which a callable bond trades is often called the yield-to-worst or the operative yield. The expected life of a bond is termed the operative life, i.e. to the call date if trading on a yield-to-call basis, or to the maturity date if trading on a yield-to-maturity basis.

A bond with a call option performs worse when interest rates change than bullet bonds maturing on the call date or the maturity date. The graph shows the price-yield curve for an 8% annual coupon, 5 year bond priced at par and callable at par after 3 years, assuming that it trades on a yield-to-worst basis.

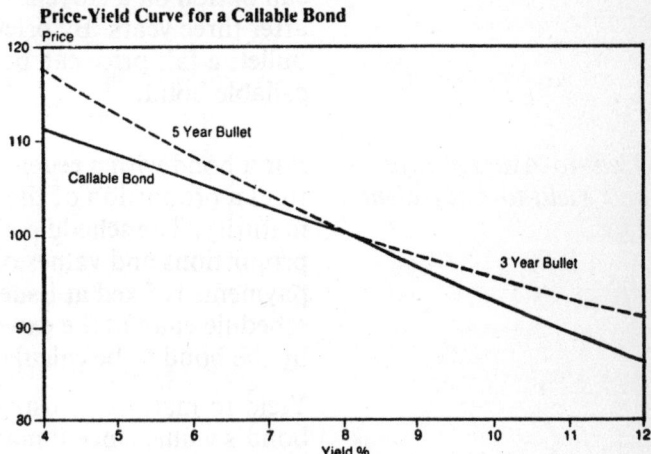

Price-Yield Curve for a Callable Bond

The callable bond combines the poor up-side performance of a 3 year bullet with the poor down-side performance of a 5 year bullet.

Yield-to-put is defined in an analogous fashion to yield to call. However, since the put is an option for the investor he will exercise it to maximise the value of the bond. Thus, a bond with a put option will trade according to the maximum of the yield-to-put and the yield-to-maturity. For example, for a 6% coupon, 5 year bond with an option to put at par after 3 years and priced at $92.01, the yield-to-put is 9.16% and the yield-to-maturity is 8%. The bond will trade according to the yield-to-put of 9.16%.

For bonds which have more than one call or put date, it is the yield to next call or next put that is usually quoted.

Finally, it is worth noting that the simple comparison of yield-to-call/put with yield-to-maturity is not a very accurate way of valuing callable/puttable bonds. CSFB has developed an approach to evaluating callable bonds using option pricing theory.* To illustrate the basic idea, consider a five year bond callable at par after three years. An investor holding such a bond can, in effect, turn it into a five year bullet by buying a call option on a current five year bullet exercisable after three years. By pricing the option and the bullet, a fair price can be calculated for the callable bond.

Yield-to-Average-Life and Yield-to-Equivalent-Life

For a bond with a redemption schedule or sinking fund a proportion of the issue is redeemed before maturity. The schedule giving the dates, proportions and values of the redemption payments is fixed at issue. Knowledge of the schedule enables the expected cash flows produced by the bond to be calculated.

Yield-to-maturity is usually a poor measure of a bond's value, since it makes the unrealistic assumption that none of the investor's holding is redeemed early.

There are two quantities which are commonly used to measure the value of a bond with a redemption schedule: yield-to-average-life and yield-to-equivalent-life, which is also called redemption yield. Yield-to-average-life is easier to calculate but does not give quite as a precise a measure of value.

---

*See 'Evaluating callable bonds', CSFB Research, September 1986.

To illustrate the calculation of these two quantities, consider a 10% annual coupon, 5 year bond priced at $107.99; its yield-to-maturity is 8%. Furthermore, suppose the bond has a redemption schedule whereby one third of the issue is redeemed after three years, one third after four years, and one third at maturity; bonds are always redeemed at par. The expected cash flows produced by the bond are shown below.

Year	% Redeemed	Coupon	Cash Flows Redemption	Total	PV at 7.60%
1	0.00	10.00	0.00	10.00	9.29
2	0.00	10.00	0.00	10.00	8.64
3	33.33	10.00	33.33	43.33	34.79
4	33.33	6.67	33.33	40.00	29.84
5	33.33	3.33	33.33	36.67	25.42
					107.99

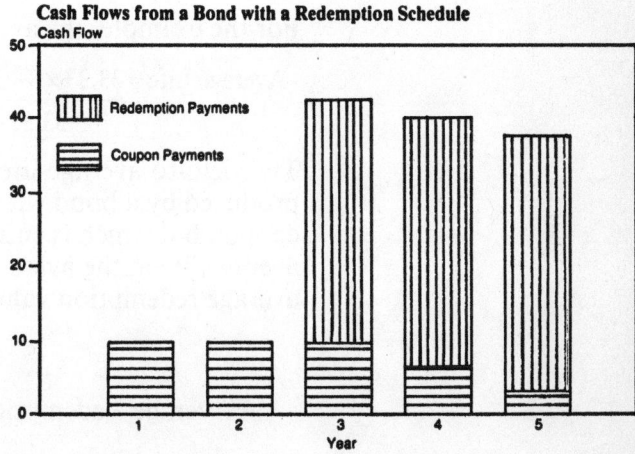

Cash Flows from a Bond with a Redemption Schedule

The average life of a bond with a redemption schedule is defined as the average redemption date weighted by the expected redemption cash flows.

$$AL = \frac{\displaystyle\sum_{i=1}^{N_r} S_i \times R_i \times T_i}{\displaystyle\sum_{i=1}^{N_r} S_i \times R_i}$$

where:
AL = Average life, years
S_i = Proportion of the outstanding issue redeemed at the ith redemption
R_i = ith redemption value. (Most commonly bonds are always redeemed at par so $R_i = 100$ for all i. However, this is not always the case.)
T_i = Number of years to the ith redemption
N_r = Number of outstanding redemptions

For the example, the average life is found to be:

$$\text{Average Life} = \frac{33.33 \times 3 + 33.33 \times 4 + 33.33 \times 5}{33.33 + 33.33 + 33.33} = 4 \text{ years}$$

The yield-to-average-life is defined as the yield produced by a bond with the same price and coupon but which is entirely redeemed on the average life at the average redemption value. The average redemption value is defined as:

$$\text{Average Redemption Value} = \sum_{i=1}^{N_r} S_i \times R_i$$

For the example, all redemptions are at par so the average redemption value is 100. Thus, the yield-to-average-life is the yield of a 4 year 10% coupon bond priced at \$107.99 and redeemed at par. This is 7.61%. It is easy to understand why this is below the yield-to-maturity. The bond is trading above par so the effect of the redemption schedule is to shorten the period over which the capital loss is incurred. This reduces the yield.

For the yield-to-equivalent-life the expected future cash flows are calculated as shown in the table above. The yield-to-equivalent-life is the yield that results in the sum of the present values of the cash flows equating to the price. This is found to be 7.60%, close to the yield-to-average-life.

The yield-to-equivalent-life is to be preferred to the yield-to-average-life as it makes allowance for the present values of redemption payments received at different times. For bonds trading at par the yield-to-average-life is very close to the yield-to-equivalent-life. The difference between them increases the further away from par the bond is trading and the longer the redemption schedule. The graph illustrates this fact for bonds with a redemption schedule which starts after 3 years and redeems in equal amounts until maturity. The plot is for a constant yield to average life of 8%.

Yield to Average Life − Yield to Equivalent Life

It is most common for sinking funds to redeem an issue in equal proportions from some start date up to maturity. If the bond pays a constant coupon and coupon periods are assumed to be of equal length, then the dirty price is related to the yield-to-equivalent-life by the formula:

$$P_d = \frac{V^K}{(1-V)} \times \left(\frac{G}{H} + \frac{V^{N-W}}{W} \times \left(100 \times (1-V^W) + \frac{G}{H} \times \frac{(V^{W+1}-V)}{(1-V)} \right) \right)$$

where:

$$V = \frac{1}{\left(1 + \dfrac{Y_q}{H \times 100} \right)}$$

Y_q = Yield-to-equivalent-life %

P_d = Dirty price

K = The fraction of a period to the next coupon payment calculated according to the appropriate market convention

G = Coupon rate %

N = Number of coupon payments outstanding

W = Number of coupon periods over which the sinking fund operates, i.e. the sinking fund starts at the $N-W+1$th coupon and ends at the Nth

H = Coupon frequency

Appendix B gives a more general version of this formula and an example of its use.

Equivalent life is a measure of the average date on which the issue is redeemed. It is defined as the weighted average of the redemption dates. The weights are the values of the expected redemption cash flows discounted by the yield-to-equivalent-life:

$$EL = \frac{\displaystyle\sum_{i=1}^{N_r} S_i \times PVCF_i \times T_i}{\displaystyle\sum_{i=1}^{N_r} S_i \times PVCF_i}$$

where:

EL = Equivalent life, years

S_i = Proportion of outstanding issue redeemed at the ith redemption

$PVCF_i$ = Present value of the ith redemption value

T_i = Number of years to the ith redemption

N_r = Number of outstanding redemptions

Note that the average life is defined similarly to equivalent life, but average life uses the actual rather than present values of the redemption payments.

In the example, the expected redemption cash flows in years 3, 4 and 5 are all 33.33. Discounting these payments at the yield-to-equivalent-life of 7.60% gives the weights 26.76, 24.87 and 23.11 respectively. The equivalent life is given by:

$$\frac{3 \times 26.76 + 4 \times 24.87 + 5 \times 23.11}{26.76 + 24.87 + 23.11} = 3.95 \text{ years}$$

The equivalent life is less than the average life of 4 years. This is always the case since using the present rather than actual values of the expected redemption cash flows gives more weight to the earlier payments. The graph shows a plot of equivalent life and average life for the example bond as a function of price. As the price increases, yield-to-equivalent-life falls so the difference in weighting between payments received at different times decreases. This means that the equivalent life tends towards the average life as the price increases.

Average Life and Equivalent Life as a Function of Price

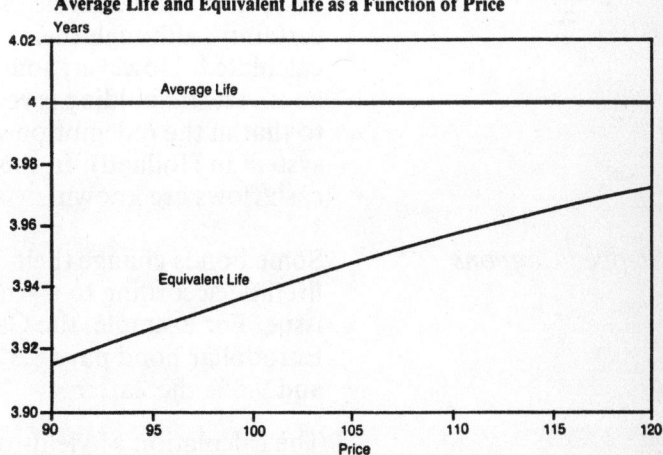

The terms of a sinking fund often allow the borrower to retire bonds by drawing or by purchases in the open market ('sinking fund by drawing or purchase'). When a bond is trading below par then the borrower may be expected to purchase in the open market if interest rates remain at current levels. In this case the yield-to-maturity gives the best measure of value. When a bond is trading above par, the borrower is likely to draw bonds for redemption, so the yield-to-equivalent-life is the appropriate measure of value. This analysis, however, does not correctly value the borrowers option (cf. callable bonds page 42).

The drawing of bonds usually takes place some time before the redemption date. Between the drawing date and the redemption date bonds are said to trade ex-redemption, i.e. the bonds being traded are ones which are not being drawn on the next redemption date. When calculating yields, the next redemption should be removed from the schedule after the drawing date.

It is worth noting that there are various ways in which the bonds due for redemption may be determined. The most commonly used method is to draw the bonds to be redeemed by lot. In this case, the future cash flows are not known with certainty, although their expected values can be calculated. However, sometimes a proportion of an investor's holding is redeemed corresponding to that in the redemption schedule (e.g. the Giro system in Holland). In this case the exact future cash flows are known.

Stepped Coupons

Some bonds change their coupon during their lifetime according to a schedule determined at issue. For example, the Garrett 8.375% 1986-96, Eurodollar bond pays 8.375% annually to 1990 and 9.5% thereafter.

The calculation of yield-to-maturity for bonds with stepped coupons is quite straightforward since the exact future cash flows are known. For example, suppose a 5 year bond pays coupons of

7%, 7.5%, 8%, 8.5%, 9% in successive years. The cash flows are shown below.

Year	CF	PV at 7.92%
1	7.00	6.49
2	7.50	6.44
3	8.00	6.36
4	8.50	6.27
5	109.00	74.45
		100.00

The yield-to-maturity is 7.92%. Not surprisingly this is less than the average coupon of 8%. The margins above 8% of the later payments have a lower present value than the corresponding margins below 8% of the earlier payments.

Partly Paid Bonds

Some bonds are issued on a partly paid basis. The investor pays part of the total price at issue and the remainder later in one or more instalments.

To calculate the yield for a partly paid bond, the future part payments must be discounted back to the settlement date.

Example
An 8% annual coupon, 5 year bond is issued on a partly paid basis with the payment schedule shown below:

At issue:	50
3 months after issue:	30
6 months after issue:	20

For partly paid bonds the first coupon payment after issue is nearly always less than usual. The calculation of the first coupon is described in 'Accrued Interest Calculations', page 79. For this example, it would be about 6.6.

The cash flows are shown in the table below.

Year	CF	PV at 8.01%
0.25	− 30.00	− 29.43
0.50	− 20.00	− 19.24
1	6.60	6.11
2	8.00	6.86
3	8.00	6.35
4	8.00	5.88
5	108.00	73.48
		50.00

The yield which equates the sum of the discounted future cash flows to the initial payment of 50 is found to be 8.01%. If the bond had been issued on a fully paid basis at par the yield would be 8%. It is usually the case that the yield of a bond issued on a partly paid basis is close to the yield of an identical bond issued fully paid at the same total price. The first coupon payment is, in effect, adjusted to cancel out the advantage to the investor of postponing part of the payment.

Indexed Bonds

For some bonds the coupon payments and/or the redemption payment are determined by the level of some index, e.g. the Retail Price Index (RPI), a stock exchange index, or a commodity index. In order to calculate the yield for such bonds, some forecast must be made for the future values of the index.

Indexed-linked gilt-edged securities provide a good example of how yields can be calculated for index-linked bonds. For index-linked gilt-edged securities both the coupon and redemption payments are linked to the RPI. The coupon payment actually received is the basic payment scaled up by a factor. This factor is the value of the RPI 8 months before the payment divided by the RPI 8 months before issue:

$$\text{Actual Payment} = \text{Basic Payment} \times \frac{\text{RPI 8 months before payment}}{\text{RPI 8 months before issue}}$$

The redemption payment is scaled in an analogous manner. The reason for using the RPI 8 months before a payment date is as follows. It is necessary to know at the start of a coupon period what the value of the coupon is going to be so that accrued interest can be calculated. Therefore, the RPI figure must be available at the start of a coupon period. Since it takes 2 months for the U.K. Government to produce RPI figures, this implies that the the RPI figure 8 months before the coupon date must be used.

The value of the next coupon is always known. To calculate subsequent payments, forecasts need to be made for the future RPI figures. The simplest approach is to assume a constant rate of inflation (the latest figure is often taken). However, if wished, more detailed forecasts of the future inflation rate can be made.

As an example of how yields can be calculated for index-linked gilt-edged securities consider 2% Index-linked 1988. This pays a basic semi-annual coupon of 2% and matures on 30th March, 1988. The RPI figure 8 months before issue was 297.1. Suppose the bond is traded for settlement on 2nd July, 1986 at a dirty price of £122.158. The next coupon is known to be £1.278. What would be its yield if a future inflation rate of 5% is assumed and the latest RPI figure is 386.0 for May, 1986?

Values of the RPI need to be forecast in order to determine future cash flows. If the inflation rate is J% per annum and the current RPI figure is RPI_c then the RPI figure M months later, RPI(M), is given by:

$$RPI(M) = RPI_c \times \left(1 + \frac{J}{100}\right)^{M/12}$$

The second coupon payment on 30th March, 1987 is determined by the RPI 8 months before, i.e. for July, 1986. This is 2 months after the latest RPI figure for May of 386.0. Therefore, the forecast RPI is:

$$RPI(2) = 386.0 \times \left(1 + \frac{5}{100}\right)^{2/12} = 389.2$$

Therefore, the forecast second coupon payment is the basic payment of £1 scaled by the ratio of the forecast RPI figure divided by the base RPI, i.e.:

$$1 \times \frac{389.2}{297.1} = £1.3098$$

Proceeding in this way, it is possible to forecast all the cash flows as shown in the table.

Date	Years from Settlement	Forecast RPI	Cash Flow	PV at 9.31%
30/9/86	0.247		1.2780	1.2496
30/3/87	0.747	389.2	1.3098	1.2238
30/9/87	1.247	398.8	1.3422	1.1982
30/3/88	1.747	408.6	138.9078	118.4867
				122.1582

The semi-annually compounded yield is found to be 9.31%. The yield calculated in this way is often called the nominal or money yield. However, in the gilt-edged market it is the real yield that is generally quoted for index-linked bonds. To convert from nominal to real yields the following formula is used:

$$R = 200 \times \left(\frac{\left(1 + \dfrac{Y}{200}\right)}{\left(1 + \dfrac{J}{100}\right)^{1/2}} - 1\right)$$

where:

R = Semi-annually compounded real yield %
Y = Semi-annually compounded nominal yield %
J = Annually compounded inflation rate %

For the example, this gives:

$$R = 200 \times \left(\frac{\left(1 + \dfrac{9.31}{200}\right)}{\left(1 + \dfrac{5}{100}\right)^{1/2}} - 1\right) = 4.27\%$$

The nominal and real yields can be calculated for a range of forecast inflation rates. The results are presented in the graph below.

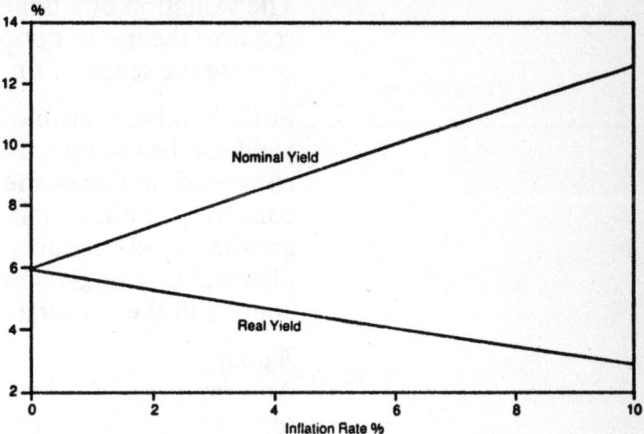

Yield against Inflation Rate for 2% Index-linked 1988

One of the reasons for the real yield being widely used stems from the belief that its value is insensitive to forecasts of the future inflation rate. As can be seen from the graph this is not the case, although for longer dated index-linked bonds, real yield is less sensitive to the inflation rate.

It might, at first glance, seem surprising that real yield decreases with increasing inflation rate. The reason for this stems from the 8 month lag in indexation. The nominal value of any payment is determined by the RPI figure 8 months previously. The real value of the payment is found by dividing the nominal value by the RPI figure at the payment date. This RPI figure will be larger than the figure 8 months previously by a factor that will increase with increasing inflation rate. Thus the real value of any payment and hence the real yield will fall with increasing inflation rate.

The formulae for the calculation of yields for index-linked gilt-edged securities are shown in Appendix C.

| Convertible Bonds | Some bonds provide the investor with the option of converting into either another bond or equity at certain times during its life. |

Some bonds provide the investor with the option of converting into either another bond or equity at certain times during its life.

The valuation of a bond convertible into equity requires the use of option pricing theory and is outside the scope of this publication.

For a bond convertible into another bond, the yield can be calculated assuming that the bond is converted on one of the conversion dates or not converted at all. A bond which is converted into another bond produces a series of cash flows identical to a single bond which changes its coupon at the conversion date.

Example
An example of a convertible bond is the gilt-edged security 9.5% Treasury Conversion 1989. This pays a semi-annual coupon on 18th April and 18th October and matures on 18th April, 1989. The investor has the option to convert the bond into 9.5% Conversion 2005 which also pays a semi-annual coupon on 18th April and 18th October and matures on 18th April, 2005. The dates and terms for the exercise of the conversion option are shown below:

Date	Amount of Conversion 9.5% 2005
18/04/85	99
18/10/85	97
18/04/86	95
18/10/86	93
18/10/87	91

The future cash flows can be calculated assuming that the bond is not converted or is converted on each of the possible conversion dates. These are shown in the table below assuming that the bond was purchased for settlement on 18th October, 1984.

| | | | Cash Flows | | | |
Date	Do not Convert	Convert 18/4/85	Convert 18/10/85	Convert 18/4/86	Convert 18/10/86	Convert 18/4/87
18/04/85	4.7500	4.7500	4.7500	4.7500	4.7500	4.7500
18/10/85	4.7500	4.7025	4.7500	4.7500	4.7500	4.7500
18/04/86	4.7500	4.7025	4.6075	4.7500	4.7500	4.7500
18/10/86	4.7500	4.7025	4.6075	4.5125	4.7500	4.7500
18/04/87	4.7500	4.7025	4.6075	4.5125	4.4175	4.7500
18/10/87	4.7500	4.7025	4.6075	4.5125	4.4175	4.3225
18/04/88	4.7500	4.7025	4.6075	4.5125	4.4175	4.3225
18/10/88	4.7500	4.7025	4.6075	4.5125	4.4175	4.3225
18/04/89	104.7500	4.7025	4.6075	4.5125	4.4175	4.3225
.		.	.	.	.	.
.		.	.	.	.	.
18/08/04		4.7025	4.6075	4.5125	4.4175	4.3225
18/04/05		103.7025	101.6075	99.5125	97.4175	95.3225
Yield at £100	9.50	9.39	9.19	9.00	8.83	8.67
Yield at £102	8.95	9.17	8.97	8.79	8.61	8.45

For each case, once the future cash flows are known, it is possible to calculate the yield. The semi-annually compounded yields are shown above when the gilt-edged security is priced at £100 and £102.

When priced at £100, the yield, if not converted, is 9.5%. If the conversion option is exercised, then the largest yield is obtained by doing so at the earliest possible date. This gives a yield of 9.39%, lower than the yield if the conversion option is not exercised. Thus, if interest rates do not subsequently change, the investor will not exercise the conversion option. Consequently, the gilt-edged security will probably trade like a short-dated bond.

When priced at £102, the largest yield is obtained by exercising the conversion option on the earliest possible date; this gives a yield of 9.17%. Thus, if interest rates do not subsequently change, the investor will exercise the conversion option as soon as possible. The gilt-edged security will probably trade like a long-dated bond, i.e. on the assumption that conversion will take place.

It is easy to understand why increasing the price sufficiently above par makes the yield if converted larger than the yield if not converted. If the bond is converted, the capital loss incurred in purchasing a bond above par is spread over a longer period, thereby lowering the yield less than when the bond is not converted. If the bond is sufficiently above par, this effect is enough to compensate the loss of yield inherent in converting at less than 100% into the longer bond.

The graph below shows the yield obtained for each of the investor's options as a function of price.

Yield against Price for 9.5% Treasury Conv 1989

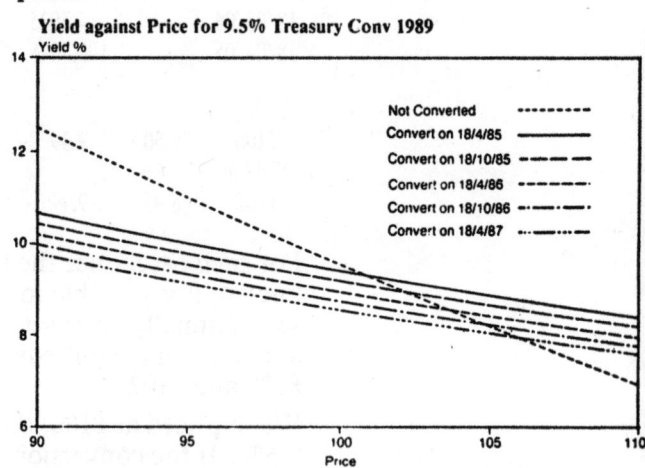

It should be noted that the method for calculating the yield of convertible bonds described above does not correctly value the options for the investor. Option pricing theory should be used.

V   Yield Related Measures

Apart from yield, there are a number of other measures which are commonly used to characterise a bond:

> Duration
> Modified Duration
> Convexity

Duration

Term to maturity is a commonly used measure of the life of a bond. However, it is a poor indicator of the timescale over which the investor receives his cash flows. A zero coupon, 5 year bond gives a single cash flow after 5 years. An 8%, 5 year bond gives a significant proportion of its total cash flow before the maturity date. The timescale of the cash flows of an 8% coupon bond is shorter than that of a zero coupon bond.

A more sophisticated measure of the length of a bond is duration. It is defined as the weighted average of the times to each of the cash flows. The weights are the present values of the cash flows. The formula for duration (often known as Macaulay duration) is:

$$D = \frac{\sum\limits_{i=1} PVCF_i \times T_i}{\sum\limits_{i=1} PVCF_i} = \frac{1}{P_d} \times \sum\limits_{i=1} PVCF_i \times T_i$$

where:

D = Duration, years

T_i = Time in years to the ith cash flow

$PVCF_i$ = Present value of the ith cash flow, i.e.

$$PVCF_i = \frac{CF_i}{\left(1 + \dfrac{Y}{100}\right)^{T_i}}$$

CF_i = ith cash flow

P_d = Dirty price

Y = Annually compounded yield %

Duration is easy to calculate for a zero coupon bond. In this case, there is only one future cash flow at T_1 with present value $PVCF_1$. Thus for a zero coupon bond:

$$D = \frac{PVCF_1 \times T_1}{PVCF_1} = T_1$$

i.e. for a zero coupon bond duration is equal to maturity. As the coupon increases more income is received earlier than the maturity date; this causes the duration to decrease. The calculation of the duration for an 8% annual coupon, 5 year bond trading at par is shown below.

T_i	CF_i	$PVCF_i$	$PVCF_i \times T_i$
1	8	7.41	7.41
2	8	6.86	13.72
3	8	6.35	19.05
4	8	5.88	23.52
5	108	73.50	367.51
		100.00	431.21

$$\text{Duration} = \frac{431.21}{100.00} = 4.31$$

Thus, the duration of the bond is 4.31 years which is less than its maturity.

Effect of Maturity and Coupon on Duration

How does the duration change with maturity? For a zero coupon bond duration always equals maturity. For a perpetual bond (infinite maturity) it can be shown that the duration is independent of the coupon and is given by:

$$D_p = \frac{100}{Y_h} + \frac{1}{H}$$

where:
D_p = Duration of a perpetual, years
Y_h = Yield compounded H times per annum %
H = Coupon frequency

The graph shows how duration varies with maturity for a zero coupon bond and bonds trading at, above and below par.

Duration against Maturity

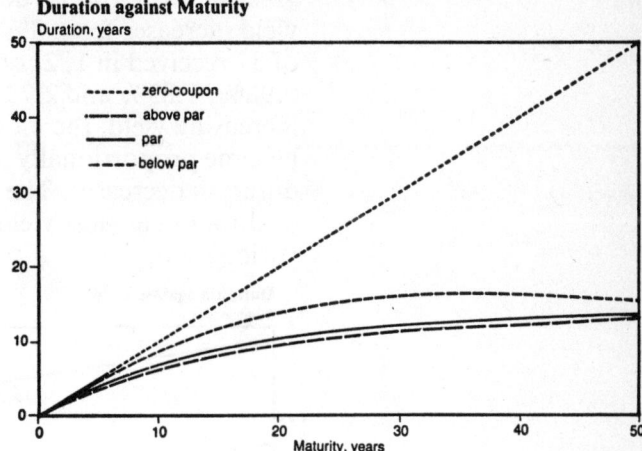

For bonds trading at or above par, the duration rises steadily towards the limiting value for a perpetual.

For a bond trading below par, the duration rises above the limiting value, reaches a maximum and then approaches the limit from above. This behaviour is easy to understand. A bond with a low coupon has a duration close to that of the zero coupon bond for low maturities since most of the return is received at maturity. However, when the maturity becomes sufficiently large, the redemption payment provides only a small proportion of the total return compared with the coupon payments. The low coupon bond then behaves like a perpetual and therefore has a duration approaching the limiting value.

Thus, for bonds trading at a discount the duration can actually decrease with maturity. However, this decrease starts at quite long maturities (about 20 years) so in practice the rule of thumb that duration increases with maturity is usually correct.

Effect of Yield on Duration

If the yield increases, then the present value of all future cash flows will decrease. However, the cash flows which are the furthest in the future show the greatest proportional decrease. For example, if the yield increases from 8% to 9%, the present values of $1 received in 1, 2, or 3 years time decrease by 0.92%, 1.83% and 2.73% respectively. Thus, for increasing yield, the more distant cash flows become proportionally less important, hence the duration decreases. The graph below shows a plot of duration against yield for a 5 year bond with various coupons.

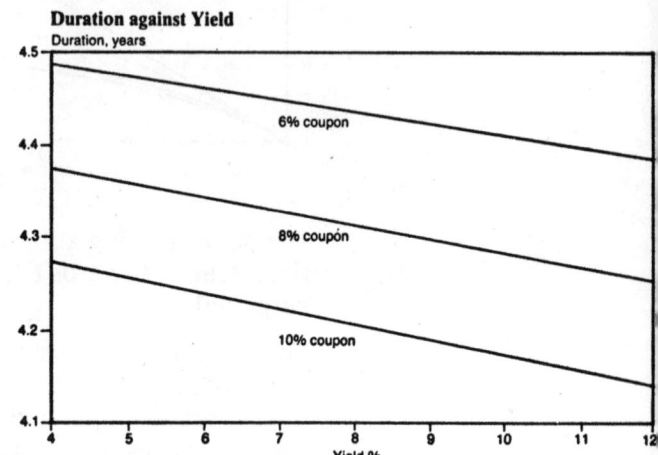

Duration as a Function of Time

The graph of duration against maturity shown on page 61 would seem to imply that, as a bond approaches maturity, its duration decreases smoothly towards zero. In fact, the graph was produced by drawing a smooth curve through the durations evaluated at each annual coupon date.

Duration does not vary smoothly with maturity. The graph below shows a plot of duration against years since issue for an 8% coupon, 20 year bond trading at par. Between coupon dates the duration decreases linearly with time but suddenly rises at a coupon date. The overall trend is a decrease in duration towards zero at the maturity date.

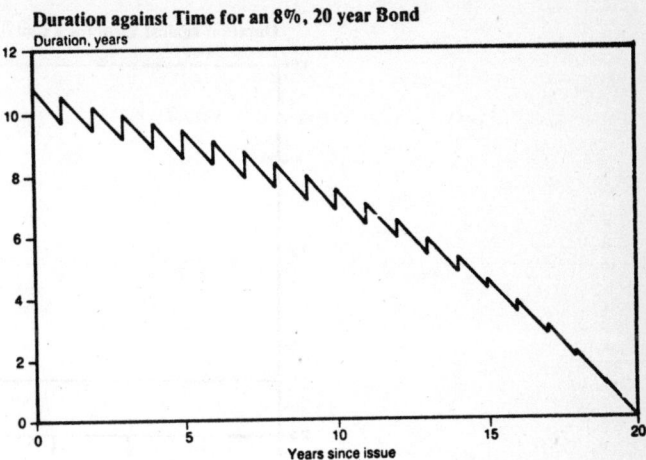

Duration against Time for an 8%, 20 year Bond

This behaviour can be understood as follows. Suppose we are between two coupon dates and a short perion of time, t, passes which still leaves us in the same coupon period. The present value of each cash flow is increased by the same factor, namely:

$$\left(1 + \frac{Y}{100}\right)^t$$

The time to all future cash flows decreases by t and, since their relative weightings stay the same, the duration decreases by t.

At a coupon date the duration increases since the dirty price suddenly falls.

Duration of Callable Bonds

Bonds which are callable show sharp changes in duration as the yield is changed. A bond priced below par will trade like a bullet maturing on the maturity date. As the price increases above par the bond will trade like a bullet maturing on the call date. This causes the duration to drop sharply.

The graph shows a plot of duration against yield for an 8% annual coupon bond, callable at par after 3 years assuming that it trades on a yield-to-worst basis.

63

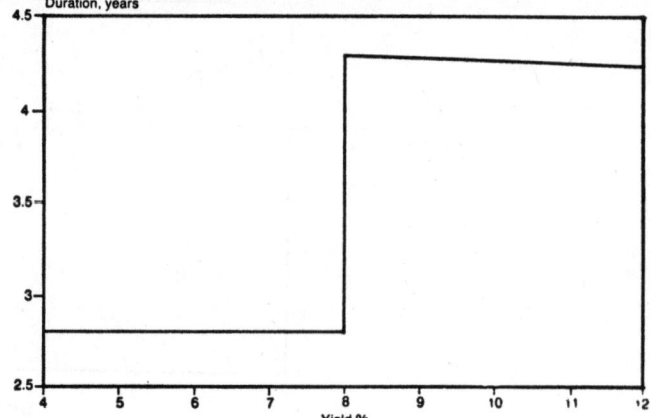

Duration against Yield for a Callable Bond
Duration, years

In practice, the duration would not show such a sudden change at the par yield. Option pricing theory predicts a more gradual change in duration.*

Modified Duration

Modified duration, which is also known as volatility in the U.K. market, is related to duration, by the formula:

$$MD = \frac{D}{\left(1 + \frac{Y_h}{H \times 100}\right)}$$

where:
MD = Modified duration, years
D = Duration, years
Y_h = Yield compounded H times per annum %
H = Coupon frequency

Example
An 8% annual coupon, 5 year bond trading at par was found to have a duration of 4.31 years. Therefore its modified duration is:

$$\text{Modified Duration} = \frac{4.31}{\left(1 + \frac{8}{100}\right)} = 3.99 \text{ years}$$

*See 'Evaluating callable bonds', CSFB Research, September 1986.

Modified duration is important because it is related to the change in price produced by a small change in yield. In fact, using straightforward mathematics, it can be shown that:

$$MD = -100 \times \frac{\Delta P_d}{\Delta Y_h} \times \frac{1}{P_d}$$

where:
MD   = Modified duration, years
P_d = Dirty price
ΔY_h = Small change in yield %
ΔP_d = Corresponding change in price

Strictly speaking, the change in yield should be infintessimally small (modified duration is related to the derivative of price with respect to yield). However, in practice, the relationship is useful for yield changes up to about 100 basis points. For example, the value of the modified duration of an 8% annual coupon, 5 year bond priced at par can be estimated using the above formula and taking various changes in yield. The results are shown below.

Change in Yield %	Estimated Modified Duration
0.001	3.99
0.01	3.99
0.1	3.98
1.0	3.89

Modified duration can be used to calculate the change in price produced by a small change in yield:

$$\Delta P_d = -0.01 \times \Delta Y_h \times MD \times P_d$$

Example
Suppose the yield of the 8% annual coupon, 5 year bond changes from 8% to 8.2%. The corresponding change in price is given approximately by:

Price Change $= -0.01 \times 0.2 \times 3.99 \times 100 = -0.80$

The exact price change is -0.79.

Uses of Duration

As described above, duration (more strictly, modified duration) gives a measure of the price change produced by a small change in yield. Bonds with high durations will exhibit greater price volatility.

Duration is important in determining optimal hedge ratios. Suppose a long position in bond L is to be hedged by selling bond S. The aim is that the value of the overall position should change as little as possible as yields vary. The problem is to determine the size of the short position which brings this about. The hedge ratio, HR, is defined as the number of bond S which should be sold for each bond L. If ΔP_s is the expected change in bond S corresponding to a price change of ΔP_l in bond L then:

$$\Delta P_l = HR \times \Delta P_s$$

Suppose the corresponding changes in yield are ΔY_l and ΔY_s, then the equation can be rewritten:

$$HR = \frac{\Delta P_l}{\Delta Y_l} \times \frac{\Delta Y_s}{\Delta P_s} \times \frac{\Delta Y_l}{\Delta Y_s}$$

If MD_l and MD_s are the modified durations of the two bonds then the equation can be further rewritten as:

$$HR = \frac{MD_l}{MD_s} \times \frac{P_l}{P_s} \times \frac{\Delta Y_l}{\Delta Y_s}$$

$\Delta Y_l / \Delta Y_s$ is the ratio of the changes in yield for the two bonds. Its value can be estimated from historical data.

As an example, suppose bond L and bond S are as below:

Bond L: 8.0% annual coupon, 5 year
        Price 100
        Yield 8.0%
        Duration 4.31 years

Bond S: 10% annual coupon, 5 year
        Price 107.99
        Yield 8.0%
        Duration 4.20 years

Since the two bonds have the same yield, the ratio of their modified durations is the same as the ratio of their durations. Taking $\Delta Y_1/\Delta Y_s$ as 1 gives the hedge ratio:

$$HR = \frac{4.31}{4.20} \times \frac{100}{107.99} = 0.95$$

Duration plays an important role in portfolio immunization. (This is discussed in 'Yield Calculations for a Portfolio' page 74.)

Convexity

Duration indicates how the price of a bond varies for small changes in yield. However, although two bonds can have the same yield and duration their behaviour under larger changes in yield can be significantly different. To illustrate this, consider the following three bonds:

Bond 1: Pays 215.8924 after 10 years
Bond 2: Pays 79.3437 after 6 years and 146.8596 after 14 years
Bond 3: Pays 58.3200 after 2 years and 199.8009 after 18 years

(Although bonds 2 and 3 have rather unlikely payment schedules, portfolios of zero-coupon bonds could be constructed which have these cash flows.)

At a yield of 8% the present values of the cash flows are:

Bond 1: PV 100 after 10 years
Bond 2: PV 50 after 6 years and 50 after 14 years
Bond 3: PV 50 after 2 years and PV 50 after 18 years

Thus, all three bonds yield 8% if priced at par. Furthermore, it is easy to see that they all have a duration of 10 years.

The graph shows how their prices change as the yield is varied.

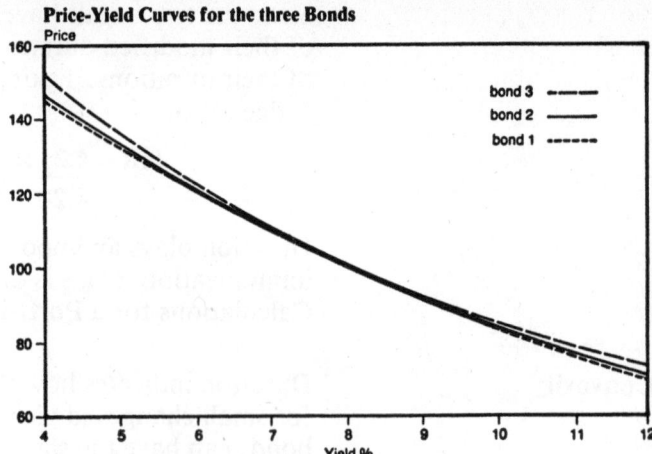

Price-Yield Curves for the three Bonds

For small changes away from the par yield, the three curves are very close to each other. However, for large yield increases or decreases the price of bond 3 lies consistently above the prices for bonds 1 and 2.

The relative superiority of bond 3 is as a result of the greater curvature of its price-yield curve. A quantity which is commonly used to measure this curvature is called convexity. It is defined in terms of the second derivative of the price with respect to yield. Details of how it is calculated are given in Appendix A.

A simple way to calculate convexity is to use the following approximation, which should be adequate for most purposes.

$$Cx = 10^8 \times \frac{1}{P_d} \times (P_p + P_m - 2 \times P_d)$$

where:

Cx = Convexity
P_d = Dirty price at the current yield
P_p = Dirty price if yield is increased by one basis point
P_m = Dirty price if yield is decreased by one basis point

Example
For Bond 1:

$P_d = 100$

$$P_p = \frac{215.8924}{\left(1 + \dfrac{8.01}{100}\right)^{10}} = 99.9074545$$

$$P_m = \frac{215.8924}{\left(1 + \dfrac{7.99}{100}\right)^{10}} = 100.0926398$$

(It is important to work to at least 7 decimal digits accuracy when calculating the prices.) The convexity for Bond 1 is therefore:

$$Cx = 10^8 \times \frac{1}{100} \times (99.9074545 + 100.0926398 - 2 \times 100) = 94$$

For the other two bonds we find:

Bond 2: Convexity = 108
Bond 3: Convexity = 149

The superior price performance of bond 3 is reflected in its higher convexity.

A better intuitive understanding of convexity is provided by the fact that it is related to the variance of the times at which cash flows are received using their present values as weights. The variance of the cash flow times, which is commonly called the dispersion, is given by the formula:

$$M^2 = \frac{1}{P_d} \times \sum_i T_i^2 \times PVCF_i - D^2$$

where:

M^2	= Dispersion
P_d	= Dirty price
D	= Duration
T_i	= Time of the ith cash flow
$PVCF_i$	= Present value of the ith cash flow

It can be shown that convexity is related to the dispersion by:

$$Cx = \cfrac{1}{\left(1 + \cfrac{Y_h}{100 \times H}\right)^2} \times \frac{(M^2 + D^2 + \underline{D})}{H}$$

where:
M^2 = Dispersion
Cx = Convexity
D = Duration
Y_h = Yield compounded H times per annum
H = Coupon frequency

It is easy to see why bond 3 has the highest convexity. Its payments are the most spread out in time, so it has the highest dispersion and hence convexity.

The relationship between convexity and dispersion provides a useful way of calculating convexity.

Example
Bond 3 pays amounts after 2 years and 18 years with the same present value of 50. The dispersion is:

$$M^2 = \frac{1}{100} \times (50 \times 2^2 + 50 \times 18^2) - 10^2 = 64$$

Therefore the convexity is given by:

$$Cx = \cfrac{1}{\left(1 + \cfrac{8}{100}\right)^2} \times (64 + 10 + 10^2) = 149$$

which agrees with the previously quoted figure.

The graph shows how convexity varies with maturity for different coupons and yields.

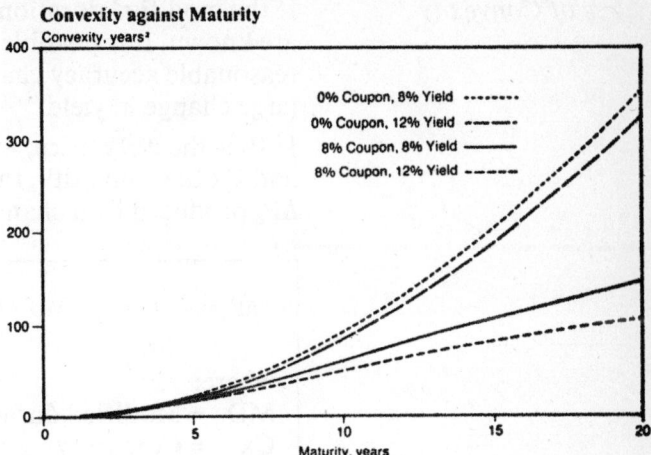

Convexity against Maturity
Convexity, years^2

Legend:
- 0% Coupon, 8% Yield ········
- 0% Coupon, 12% Yield – – – –
- 8% Coupon, 8% Yield ——
- 8% Coupon, 12% Yield – – – –

Maturity, years

For zero coupon bonds the duration equals the maturity. The relationship between convexity, dispersion and duration shows that convexity will increase as the square of the maturity.

For a bond paying a coupon, duration reaches an upper limit as the maturity increases. Therefore convexity does not increase so rapidly as the maturity increases.

As the yield increases convexity decreases slightly.

Convexity shows how duration varies with yield. Positive convexity implies that as the yield increases the duration decreases. Negative convexity implies that as the yield increases the duration increases.

For securities in which the future cash flows are independent of yield levels the convexity is positive. This is the case for non-callable bonds.

For callable bonds the duration sharply increases when the yield moves above the par yield. Thus, the convexity is negative for a callable bond round about the par yield. Mortgage-backed securities also exhibit negative convexity. As yields fall pre-payment increases and so the duration falls.

From the investor's point of view a large postitve convexity is desirable.

Uses of Convexity

If the modified duration and convexity of a bond are known, it is possible to calculate with reasonable accuracy changes in the price for a large change in yield.

If P_d is the dirty price, MD the modified duration and Cx the convexity, then the change in price, ΔP_d produced by a change in yield, $\Delta Y\%$ is given by:

$$\Delta P_d = -\frac{1}{100} \times P_d \times MD \times \Delta Y_h + \frac{1}{2} \times P_d \times \frac{Cx}{10000} \times \Delta Y_h^2$$

where:
MD $\quad$= Modified duration
Cx $\quad$= Convexity
P_d $\quad$= Dirty price
ΔY_h $\quad$= Change in yield %
ΔP_d $\quad$= Change in price

Example
For bond 3, the modified duration can be calculated:

$$MD = \frac{D}{\left(1 + \dfrac{Y_h}{100 \times H}\right)} = \frac{10}{\left(1 + \dfrac{8}{100}\right)} = 9.26$$

If the yield increases from 8% to 10%, the change in price using the above formula is:

$$\Delta P_d = -\frac{1}{100} \times 100 \times 9.26 \times 2 + \frac{1}{2} \times 100 \times \frac{149}{10000} \times 2^2 = -15.54$$

If the term involving the convexity is omitted from the formula the price increment is -18.52. The exact increment in price is -15.87. Clearly, using convexity as well as duration to compute the price change produced by a large yield change gives more accurate results.

Convexity is an important consideration when constructing hedged positions. The aim is that the total value of of the hedged position be insensitive to yield changes. This can partially be achieved by taking up a short position whose size is given by the hedge ratio described in 'Uses of Duration', page 66. However, for larger yield changes the value of a hedged position can vary significantly. As an example, consider the following two postions with both bonds yielding 8%.

Position 1: Long one Bond 1, short one Bond 3
Position 2: Short one Bond 1, long one Bond 3

Since both bonds have the same price and duration the hedge ratio is unity and both postions are correctly hedged. The graph shows how the value of the two positions vary with yield.

Value of Hedged Positions against Yield

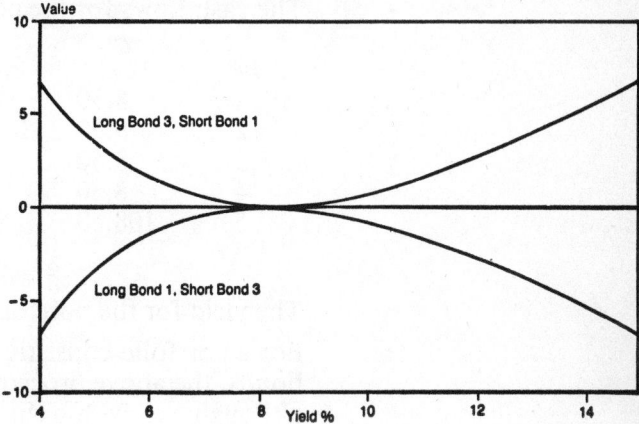

A holder of position 1 would make a loss if yields moved away from 8%. Conversely, a holder of position 2 make a gain if yields shifted.

The good performance of position 2 comes about because bond 3 has a higher convexity than bond 1. In general, when constructing a hedged position one should try to ensure that the long position has a greater convexity than the short position.

If HR is the hedge ratio, P_l and P_s the prices, and C_l and C_s the convexities of the bonds in the long and short postions respectively, one should try to ensure that:

$$HR \times \frac{P_s}{P_l} \times \frac{C_s}{C_l} \leqslant 1$$

VI Yield Calculations for a Portfolio

Yield of a Portfolio

The calculation of the yield for a portfolio of bonds is similar to the calculation for a single bond. The future cash flows produced by the portfolio are calculated and the yield found which equates the sum of their present values to the current market value of the portfolio.

As a simple example, consider a portfolio constructed from equal amounts of two bonds:

Bond 1: 8.5% annual coupon, 5 year, price par.
       Yield 8.5%
Bond 2: 8.0% annual coupon, 2 year, price par.
       Yield 8.0%

The cash flows for the portfolio are shown below:

Year	CF Bond 1	CF Bond 2	CF Portfolio	PV at 8.35%
1	8.50	8.00	8.25	7.61
2	8.50	108.00	58.25	49.62
3	8.50	0.00	4.25	3.34
4	8.50	0.00	4.25	3.08
5	108.50	0.00	54.25	36.34
				100.00

The yield for the portfolio is 8.35%.

For a portfolio consisting of a large number of bonds, the above procedure is rather laborious, although well within the capabilities of a computer. For this reason, the yield of a portfolio is sometimes calculated by taking the weighted average of the yields of the bonds in the portfolio. The weights are the market values using dirty prices, i.e.

$$APY = \frac{\sum_i MV_i \times Y_i}{\sum_i MV_i}$$

where:

APY = Average portfolio yield
MV_i = Market value of ith bond including accrued interest, i.e. dirty price × nominal amount held/100
Y_i = Yield of ith bond

For the two bond portfolio, this gives a yield of 8.25%, 10 basis points less than the precisely calculated yield.

It can be shown that a more accurate value for the yield of a portfolio is obtained by taking the weighted average of the yields using the market value times duration as weights, i.e.

$$DWPY = \frac{\sum_i D_i \times MV_i \times Y_i}{\sum_i D_i \times MV_i}$$

where:
DWPY = Duration weighted portfolio yield
MV_i = Market value of the ith bond including accrued interest, i.e. dirty price × nominal amount held/100
D_i = Duration of the ith bond
Y_i = Yield of the ith bond

The duration of bond 1 is found to be 4.28 years, that of bond 2 is 1.93 years. Therefore:

$$DWPY = \frac{8.5 \times 4.28 + 8.0 \times 1.93}{4.28 + 1.93} = 8.34$$

The duration weighted portfolio yield is within one basis point of the precisely calculated portfolio yield.

The duration weighted portfolio yield will be most accurate if the range of individual bond yields is narrow.

Finally, it should be noted that it is only meaningful to compute the weighted average of bond yields to get the portfolio yield if the yields are all calculated on the same basis. If, for example, some yields are compounded semi-annually and some annually, then the weighted average yield is a meaningless figure.

Duration of a Portfolio

The duration of a portfolio can be calculated in a similar manner to a single bond. The times and amounts of future cash flows are computed and the yield calculated as described above. The duration is then the weighted average of the payment times using the present values of the payments, discounted at the portfolio yield, as weights. For the example two bond portfolio, this gives a duration of 3.11 years.

In practice, to determine the duration of a portfolio, it is common to compute the weighted average of the durations of the bonds using the market values as weights, i.e.:

$$APD = \frac{\sum_i D_i \times MV_i}{\sum_i MV_i}$$

where:
APD = Average portfolio duration
D_i = Duration of the ith bond
MV_i = Market value of the ith bond including accrued interest, i.e. dirty price $\times$ nominal amount held/100

For the two bond portfolio, this gives a duration of 3.10 years, close to the precise value of 3.11 years.

Strictly speaking, to calculate the duration of a portfolio the precise method should be used. The average portfolio duration would give the correct answer if all the durations for the bonds were calculated at the portfolio yield. Since the durations will, in general, be calculated for different yields, a correction needs to be made. In practice, the error introduced by ignoring this correction is very small and, as the example illustrates, the average portfolio duration is accurate enough.

Uses of the Duration of a Portfolio

Duration plays an important role in portfolio managment. Duration can be used to calculate the change in market value of a portfolio produced by a small change in yield. This is done in the same way as for a single bond.

Duration is important in portfolio immunization. An immunized portfolio is a portfolio held for a specific period and managed in such a way that, regardless of the course of interest rates, the return at the end of the holding period is at least as large as the portfolio yield at the start of the period.

It can be shown that a portfolio is immunized if its duration is matched to the investment horizon *throughout* the holding period.

Convexity of a Portfolio

The convexity of a portfolio is calculated as the weighted average of the convexities of the bonds using the market values as weights, i.e.

$$APC = \frac{\sum_i Cx_i \times MV_i}{\sum_i MV_i}$$

where:
APC = Average portfolio convexity
Cx_i = Convexity of the ith bond
MV_i = Market value of the ith bond including accrued interest, i.e. dirty price × nominal amount held/100

This method of calculation is not strictly correct (cf. 'Duration of a Portfolio', page 76), but is sufficiently accurate in practice.

Ideally, the convexity of a portfolio should be as large as possible. In practice, however, if the duration is fixed, there tends to be a trade-off between convexity and yield.

VII General Features of the Bond Markets

Coupon Dates

Most fixed interest bonds pay interest annually, semi-annually or quarterly, although a few bonds have been issued with other payment frequencies. Interest payments occur on fixed days, the appropriate number of months apart. For example, a bond paying interest quarterly might have coupon dates of 13th February, 13th May, 13th August and 13th November.

Coupon payments usually occur at fixed intervals apart. However, it is not uncommon for the interval between the issue date and the first coupon date and/or the interval between the last full coupon payment and redemption to be of non-standard lengths.

It should be noted that these scheduled coupon dates are nominal in the sense that if one happens to fall on a non-business day, payment will actually take place on the next business day.

A complication occurs with bonds paying more than one coupon per annum and which have a maturity date on the last day of a month. There are two approaches that are commonly used for determining when the payment dates occur:

— Payment dates on the last days of the appropriate months. This is the usual approach in the U.S. market. For example the U.S. Treasury Note 12.25% maturing on 30th September, 1986 has coupon dates on 31st March and 30th September.

— Payment dates are on the same day of the appropriate month. Obviously the issuer would have ensured that these dates actually exist. This is the usual approach in the U.K. market. For example, the U.K. gilt-edged security 15.5% maturing on 30th September, 1998 has coupon dates on 30th March and 30th September.

In the descriptions of the individual market sectors given below any peculiarities about coupon payments are noted.

Price Quotations

Prices are usually quoted clean, excluding any accrued interest. In a few cases dirty prices are quoted, for example:

> French domestic indexed bonds;
> U.K. and Irish bonds settled for account;
> Spanish domestic bonds.

Accrued Interest Calculations

The price a buyer has to pay for a bond is the clean price (usually the same as the quoted price) plus any accrued interest. If the buyer receives the next coupon, the bond is said to be traded cum-dividend or cum-coupon and the accrued interest is positive. If the buyer forgoes the next coupon, the bond is said to be traded ex-dividend or ex-coupon and the accrued interest is negative.

In some markets (e.g. U.S.) bonds are always traded cum-dividend. In other markets for a certain period before a coupon date, bonds are traded ex-dividend.

Interest accrues on a bond from and including the date of the previous coupon up to but excluding a date called the value date. The value date is usually, but not invariably, the same as the settlement date. Unlike the settlement date, the value date is not constrained to fall on a business day.

It is important to note that the term 'value date' is not used consistently in different markets. The definition of value date given above is that used by the Association of International Bond Dealers (AIBD). It is also the definition used in all the market descriptions in this publication. However, in some markets interest accrues up to *and including* a date which is referred to as the value date. Thus the market descriptions may, at a first glance, differ from the commonly stated market practice.

What constitutes the 'next coupon' is not as simple as it might at first seem. Most commonly the next coupon is determined with reference to

79

the value date. If the value date is on a coupon date, then the next coupon is the following one. However, in the Swiss market the next coupon is determined with respect to the trade date. In the German market the procedure is more complicated. In the market descriptions it is assumed that the next coupon is determined with reference to the value date unless otherwise stated.

The accrued interest on a bond traded cum-dividend is the interest which has accrued between the previous coupon date and the value date.

The accrued interest on a bond traded ex-dividend is minus the interest which would accrue between the value date and the next coupon date.

When calculating accrued interest, it is generally the case that a coupon payment is assumed to take place on the scheduled date even if it will be delayed if this date is a non-business day.

Firstly, it will be shown how to calculate the accrued interest in a normal length coupon period on a fully paid bond. The complications of abnormal coupon periods and part payments are dealt with later in this section.

The interest accrued between two dates in the same coupon period is calculated using simple interest:

$$AI = \frac{d}{A_y} \times G$$

where:
AI = Accrued interest
d = Number of days between the two dates
A_y = Assumed number of days in a year
G = Coupon rate %

The way in which d and A_y are calculated is market dependent. The most common methods for calculating d are:

1) (denoted 'ACT')
Calculating the actual number of days between the two dates.

2) (denoted '30')
Calculating the number of days between the two dates assuming 30 day months using the following calculation procedure. The number of days between the dates $D_1/M_1/Y_1$ and $D_2/M_2/Y_2$ is given by:

If D_1 is 31 change to 30.

If D_2 is 31 and D_1 is 30 or 31 change D_2 to 30 otherwise leave at 31.

Then the number of days between the two dates is given by:

$$(Y_2 - Y_1) \times 360 + (M_2 - M_1) \times 30 + (D_2 - D_1)$$

Thus there are 29 days between 1st May and 30th May, 30 days between 1st May and 31st May.

3) (denoted '30E')
Calculating the number of days between the two dates assuming 30 day months using the following calculation procedure. The number of days between the dates $D_1/M_1/Y_1$ and $D_1/M_2/Y_2$ is given by:

If D_1 is 31 change to 30.

If D_2 is 31 change to 30.

Then the number of days between the two dates is given by:

$$(Y_2 - Y_1) \times 360 + (M_2 - M_1) \times 30 + (D_2 - D_1)$$

Thus there are 29 days between 1st May and 30th May, 29 days between 1st May and 31st May.

This method is used in the Euromarkets and some continental domestic markets.

The most common methods for calculating A_y are:

1) (denoted '365')
Assume a year of 365 days.

2) (denoted 'ACT')
Take A_y to be the number of days in the current coupon period multiplied by the number of coupon payments per annum. For a semi-annual coupon, the number of days in a coupon period can range from 181 to 184 so A_y ranges from 362 to 368.

3) (denoted '360')
Assume a year of 360 days.

For bonds calculating d on a '30' or '30E' basis, there is another, almost equivalent, way of looking at this. One can define A_y as the number of days in a coupon period working on a '30' or '30E' basis multiplied by the number of coupon payments per annum. For a bond with coupons falling either on fixed days of the month or at the end of the month this will usually give $A_y = 360$.

The exception is for an annual bond paying at the end of February, or a semi-annual bond paying at the end of February and the end of August. For example for a semi-annual bond paying on 28/29th February and 31st August then A_y can be 356, 358, 364 or 366 working on a '30' basis.

In this exceptional case for many markets which use the '30' or '30E' method combined with a 360 day year it is not clear what should be done. In the U.S. A_y is calculated on the basis of the number of days in the coupon period. In the Euromarkets, however, issuers have avoided this exceptional case (the AIBD rule book recommends issuers to avoid it) so the right procedure to use has not been defined.

In the descriptions of the market conventions, the accrued interest calculation method is denoted by 'd method'/'A_y method' e.g. ACT/365, 30E/360. Of the nine possible combinations of 'd method' and 'A_y method', there are only 5 that occur in practice: ACT/365, ACT/360, 30/360, 30E/360, and ACT/ACT.

Example

Consider a bond whose last coupon was on 1st May, 1986 and whose next coupon falls on 1st November, 1986. The number of days in the current coupon period is 184. The accrued interest as a proportion of the coupon is shown for each of the methods for the value dates 30th May, 31st May and 1st June.

	30th May	Value Date 31st May	1st Jun
ACT/365	29/365	30/365	31/365
ACT/360	29/360	30/360	31/360
30/360	29/360	30/360	30/360
30E/360	29/360	29/360	30/360
ACT/ACT	29/368	30/368	31/368

Example

The U.K. gilt-edged security 9.75% Conversion 2001 is traded for settlement on the 2nd July, 1986. The previous coupon was on the 10th February, 1986, and the next coupon on the 10th August, 1986. In the U.K. domestic market, interest accrues on an ACT/365 basis. The value date is the same as the settlement date. A particular feature of the U.K. market means that the bond can be traded cum or ex-dividend (see page 102).

There are 142 days from the previous coupon to the settlement date. Therefore, if the bond is traded cum-dividend, the accrued interest is:

$$\frac{142 \times 9.75}{365} = 3.793$$

There are 39 days from the settlement date to the next coupon. If the bond is traded ex-dividend the accrued interest is:

$$\frac{-39 \times 9.75}{365} = -1.042$$

There are 181 days in the current coupon period. If interest were accrued for this whole period, it would amount to:

$$\frac{181}{365} \times 9.75 = 4.835$$

Note that this is not exactly the same as the next coupon payment of 4.875.

Example
The U.S. Treasury bond 6.75% 1993 is traded for settlement on the 2nd July, 1986. The previous coupon was on 15th February, 1986, and the next coupon on 15th August, 1986. Interest accrues on an ACT/ACT basis. Bonds are always traded cum-dividend in the U.S. market. The value date is the same as the settlement date.

There are 181 days in the current coupon period. There are 137 days from the previous coupon to the settlement date. Therefore, the accrued interest is:

$$\frac{137}{2 \times 181} \times 6.75 = 2.555$$

Note that, in contrast to the previous example, the accrued interest for the whole coupon period is the same as the next coupon payment.

Abnormal Coupon Periods

It is not uncommon for the first coupon period after issue to be of abnormal length. If the first coupon payment is shorter/longer than usual then the first coupon payment will be smaller/larger than usual. Usually, the first coupon payment is the same as the interest that would accrue from issue up to the first coupon date.

With the exception of bonds using the ACT/ACT method, accrued interest can still be calculated as described above.

Example
The U.K. gilt-edged security 2.5% Exchequer 1990 was issued on the 22nd January, 1986. Coupon payments are semi-annual on 22nd May

and 22nd November. The first coupon period is therefore short. Interest accrues on an ACT/365 basis. The value date is the same as the settlement date.

The first coupon payment is the interest that accrues between the issue date and the first coupon date on 22nd May, 1986. There are 120 actual days in the first coupon period. Therefore the first coupon is:

$$\frac{120}{365} \times 2.5 = 0.8219$$

Suppose the bond is traded for settlement on the 13th February, 1986. This is 22 actual days from issue. Therefore the accrued interest is:

$$\frac{22}{365} \times 2.5 = 0.1507$$

For bonds using the ACT/ACT method (U.S. Treasuries) a slightly modified procedure must be used.

If the first coupon period is shorter than usual, accrued interest is still calculated on the basis of a year of A_y days. However, in this case A_y is the number of days between the issue date for a normal period and the next coupon date multiplied by the coupon frequency.

Example
The U.S. Treasury 6.125% maturing 31st August, 1988 was issued on 2nd September, 1986. Coupon payments are semi-annual on 31st August and 28/29th February. Interest accrues on an ACT/ACT basis.

The first coupon period from 2nd September, 1986 to 28th February, 1987 is short, consisting of 179 actual days. For a normal coupon period the bond would have been issued on the 31st August, 1986 giving a coupon period of 181 actual days and hence $A_y = 2 \times 181 = 362$. Therefore, the first coupon payment is the interest accrued between issue and the first coupon date:

$$\frac{179}{362} \times 6.125 = 3.0287$$

If the first coupon period is long, the period is regarded as being broken up into two segments:

— The first segment runs from the issue date to the missing payment date, i.e. the date 6 months before the first coupon. In this segment, interest accrues as for a short period with the first coupon falling on the missing payment date.

— The second segment runs from the missing payment date to the first payment date. In this segment, interest accrues as if it were a normal coupon period.

Example

The U.S. Treasury 7.25% maturing on 15th July, 1993 was issued on the 7th July, 1986. Coupon payments are semi-annual on 15th January and 15th July. The first coupon period from 7th July, 1986 to 15th January, 1987 is long, consisting of 192 days. Suppose the bond is traded for settlement on the 30th August, 1986. To calculate the accrued interest, proceed as follows:

The long period is divided up into two segments as described above. The missing payment date is 6 months before the first coupon date, i.e. 15th July, 1986. The first segment is treated as a short coupon period running from the 7th July, 1986 to the 15th July, 1986, i.e. 8 days. The issue date would have to be on the 15th January, 1986 to make this a normal period of 181 days with $A_y = 362$. Therefore, the interest accrued in the first segment is:

$$\frac{8}{362} \times 7.25 = 0.1602$$

The second segment is handled as a normal coupon period running from 15th July, 1986 to 15th January, 1987, i.e. 184 days so $A_y = 368$. Interest is accrued from 15th July, 1986 to 30th August, 1986, i.e. 46 days. Therefore the accrued interest for this segment is:

$$\frac{46}{368} \times 7.25 = 0.9063$$

The total interest accrued is the sum of the interest accrued in the two segments, i.e.

$$0.1602 + 0.9063 = 1.0665$$

Partly Paid Bonds

Some bonds are issued in partly paid form, the balance being paid in instalments before the first coupon date. This is particularly common in the U.K. sterling market. Whilst a bond is partly paid, it accrues interest at a fraction of the rate of a fully paid bond. This fraction is either:

a) The amount paid so far divided by the issue price; or

b) The amount paid so far divided by par.

Which method is used depends on the market. For example, in the U.K. gilt-edged market the former method is used, the issue price being the minimum tender price. In the Euromarkets the latter method is used.

The first coupon of a partly paid bond is non-standard and is equal to the total interest that accrues between the issue and first coupon dates.

Example
The U.K. gilt-edged security 10% Treasury 2003 was issued at a minimum tender price of 93.5 on a partly paid basis on 24th January, 1986. The initial payment was 35 and the balance of 58.5 was due on 14th April, 1986. The first coupon date was 8th September, 1986. In the U.K. domestic market interest accrues on an ACT/365 basis. For partly paid bonds method a) is used.

To calculate the first coupon, proceed as follows. Between 24th January, 1986 and 14th April, 1986 there are 80 actual days. For this period the bond is:

$$\frac{35}{93.5} \times 100 = 37.43\%$$

paid up. During this period, interest accrues at 37.43% of the rate it would do if fully paid up. Therefore the interest accrued during this period is:

$$\frac{37.43}{100} \times \frac{80}{365} \times 10 = 0.8205$$

Between 14th April, 1986 and 8th September, 1986 there are 147 actual days. During this period the bond is fully paid so the accrued interest is:

$$\frac{147}{365} \times 10 = 4.0274$$

The first coupon is the total interest accrued between the issue and first coupon date, i.e.

$$0.8205 + 4.2074 = 4.8479$$

Suppose the bond was traded for settlement on 3rd March, 38 days after issue and before the second payment is due. Interest has accrued for 38 days on a 37.43% paid basis. Therefore the accrued interest is:

$$\frac{37.43}{100} \times \frac{38}{365} \times 10 = 0.3897$$

Bonds redeemed in between Coupons

If a bond is called by the issuer between coupon dates, the holder receives the interest accrued up to the redemption date as well as the redemption payment.

Fractional Coupon Periods and Accrued Interest Calculation

In the section 'Fractional Coupon Periods', page 30, the method is described that is commonly used to discount payments received a fractional number of coupon periods from settlement. $1 received after $N + K$ coupon periods has the present value:

$$\frac{\$1}{\left(1 + \dfrac{Y_h}{H \times 100}\right)^{N+K}}$$

where Y_h is the yield compounded H times per annum, N is the number of whole periods to the payment and K is the fraction of a period left over.

It is common to calculate K in the same way as for accrued interest in the market. The interest accrued between settlement and the next coupon payment is:

$$\frac{d_{sn} \times G}{A_y}$$

where d_{sn} is the number of days between settlement and the next coupon and A_y is the number of days in a year, both quantities being calculated on the appropriate market basis. The fraction of a period to the first coupon is then given by:

$$K = \frac{d_{sn} \times H}{A_y}$$

Appendix B gives formulae for yields calculated according to this method.

Example
The Eurodollar bond, Industrial Bank of Japan, 10.875% annual coupon maturing on 25th April, 1988 is traded for settlement on 29th August, 1986 at a clean price of 106.75. In the Euromarkets interest accrues on a 30E/360 basis. The value date is the same as the settlement date.

First calculate the accrued interest. The previous coupon payment was on 25th April, 1986 so there are 124 days accrued interest working on the basis of a 30 day month. Therefore, the accrued interest is:

$$\frac{124 \times 10.875}{360} = 3.746$$

Quoted yields for Eurobonds are usually calculated using the AIBD method. This method assumes equal length coupon periods and calculates fractional periods in the same way as for accrued interest. The number of days from settlement to the next coupon is 236 working on the basis of a 30 day month. Therefore, K is given by:

$$K = \frac{236}{360} = 0.656$$

There are two payments outstanding: 10.875 after 0.656 periods and 110.875 after 1.656 periods. Therefore, the annually compounded yield, Y_a, is the solution to the equation:

$$106.75 + 3.746 = \frac{10.875}{\left(1 + \frac{Y_a}{100}\right)^{0.656}} + \frac{110.875}{\left(1 + \frac{Y_a}{100}\right)^{1.656}}$$

The solution is $Y_a = 6.40\%$.

For a bond priced at par the yield is equal to the coupon only at coupon dates. Between coupon dates the yield is less than the coupon, the difference becoming greater the shorter the maturity. The graph shows a plot of yield against maturity for an 8% annual coupon bond priced at par.

Yield of an 8% Coupon Bond Priced at Par

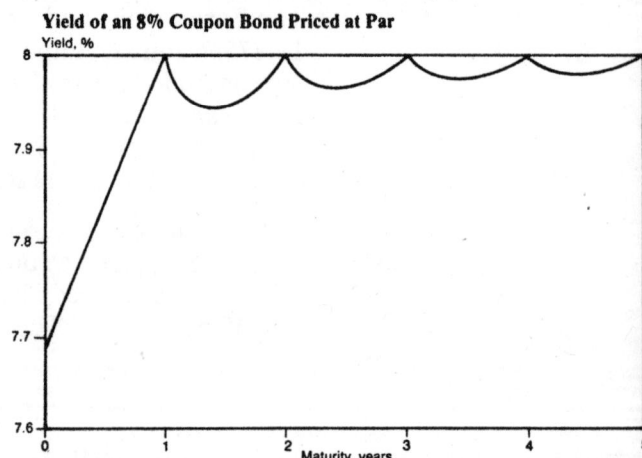

The reason for this variation in yield arises from the fact that interest accrues on a bond according to simple interest, whilst the fractional coupon period is discounted using compound interest.

VIII Market Details

AUSTRIAN MARKET

Money Market Instruments

Yields and discounts are quoted on an ACT/360 basis.

Domestic Bonds

Austrian bonds pay an annual coupon.

Coupon Dates
Value and Settlement Dates

Bonds are traded for settlement on the next Monday but one after the trade date, e.g.:

Trade Date	Settlement Date
Mon 6th Oct	Mon 20th Oct
Tue 7th Oct	Mon 20th Oct
Fri 10th Oct	Mon 20th Oct
Mon 13th Oct	Mon 27th Oct

If the Monday is a non-business day, then settlement is on the next business day.

The value date is the same as the settlement date.

Interest Accrual

Interest accrues on a 30E/360 basis.

Ex-Dividend Dates

The ex-dividend date is the first Monday in a month if the next coupon date is between the 10th and the 24th of the same month, and the first Monday after the 14th of a month if the next coupon date is between the 25th of the same month and the 9th of the following month.

A bond is traded ex-dividend if the settlement date falls on or after the ex-dividend date.

Market Yield Calculations

Yields quoted by the stock exchange are calculated using the AIBD method (see page 108).

BELGIAN MARKET

Money Market Instruments

Yields and discounts are quoted on an ACT/365 basis.

Domestic Bonds

Belgian bonds are not traded ex-dividend.

Coupon Dates

Belgian bonds pay an annual coupon.

Value and Settlement Dates

The settlement date is two business days after the trade date. The value date is the day following the day which is one business day after the trade date. Thus if the trade date is a Thursday, then the value date is on the Saturday and the settlement date on the Monday.

Interest Accrual

Interest accrues an a 30E/360 basis. The buyer usually pays to the seller the gross accrued interest less 25% withholding tax. The exception is for issues of supranational debtors, in which case the gross accrued interest is paid.

Market Yield Calculations

Yields quoted by the Stock Exchange are calculated on the following basis:

— For gross yields allowance is still made for the 25% withholding tax by assuming that the buyer pays to the seller the gross accrued interest less 25% withholding tax. However, the first coupon payment he receives is reduced by the amount of tax on the accrued interest.

— For net yields all interest payments (accrued and coupon) are reduced by 25%.

For bonds with more than one coupon to maturity the AIBD method is used (see page 108).

For bonds in their final coupon period yields are calculated using simple interest on an ACT/365 basis.

DUTCH MARKET

Money Market Instruments

Yields and discounts can either be quoted on an ACT/360 or a 30E/360 basis.

Domestic and Foreign Bonds

Most issues in the Dutch market have sinking funds. In the new Giro system the appropriate proportion of an investor's holding is redeemed at each redemption date. This replaced the previous system of drawing by lot.

A few Dutch Government bonds are convertible before the first redemption date at the user's option into an equal nominal amount of a longer dated bond.

A large percentage of the domestic market consists of private placements (Onderhandse Leningen).

Coupon Dates

Most domestic and foreign bonds pay interest annually, a few semi-annually.

Value and Settlement Dates

The value and settlement dates are usually the same as the trade date.

Interest Accrual

Interest accrues on a 30E/360 basis.

Ex-Dividend Dates

Bonds go ex-dividend 14 days before the nominal coupon date.

Market Yield Calculations

Quoted yields are calculated using the AIBD method (see page 108). However, for bonds with sinking funds the yield-to-equivalent-life rather than the yield-to-average-life is quoted. Annually compounded yields are always quoted. For convertible Government bonds the yield if not converted and the yield if converted are both quoted.

GERMAN MARKET

The German market can be divided into the following sectors:

Money Market Instruments
Domestic and Foreign Bonds
Schuldscheindarlehen

Money Market Instruments

The discounts and yields of money market instruments are quoted on an ACT/360 basis.

Domestic and Foreign Bonds

There is a wide variety of fixed interest instruments issued in the German domestic and foreign markets. Issues include:

— Bonds issued by the Federal Government, the Federal Railway, and the Federal Post Office, collectively known as Bundbahnpost bonds.

— Kassenobligationen issued by the Federal and state governments with maturities of six months to four years.

— Non-interest bearing U-Schaetze.

— Laenderanleihen, or state bonds.

— Pfandbriefe, or mortgage bonds, issued by banks to finance mortgage loans.

— Kommunalobligationen issued by banks to finance municipal loans.

— Industrial bonds.

Some issues have a redemption schedule in which one or more tranches of the original issue are redeemed. About one month's notice is given that a particular tranche is going to be redeemed. During the period up to redemption a tranche that is about to be redeemed may trade differently from one that is not.

Coupon Dates

Most bonds pay interest annually, a few semi-annually.

Value and Settlement Dates

The value date is usually 2 business days after the trade date. The settlement date is the same as the value date.

However, it is quite common for banks outside Germany to trade domestic German bonds on the same basis as the Euromarkets with value and settlement dates 7 days after the trade date (see page 108).

Interest Accrual

Interest accrues on a 30E/360 basis.

Ex-Dividend Dates

The rules of the security-clearing association (Kassenverein) are quite complicated for determining ex-dividend dates and whether the accrued interest is positive or negative. With effect from 1st July, 1986 the rules are as follows.

If the next coupon date is between the 3rd and 16th of a month, then the ex-dividend date is the first business day after the last day of the previous month. If the next coupon date is between the 17th of the current month and the 2nd of the next month then the ex-dividend date is the first business day after the 15th of the current month.

Accrued interest is positive if:

— The trade date is before the ex-dividend date. The buyer receives the next coupon following the trade date. Accrued interest is calculated from the previous coupon date to the value date. Note that in this case it is possible to have more than 360 days accrued interest.

— The trade date is the ex-dividend date or later and the day before the settlement date is in the new coupon period. The buyer does not receive the next coupon following the trade date but receives the one after that. Accrued interest is calculated from the next coupon date to the value date.

Accrued interest is negative if:

— The trade date is the ex-dividend date or later and the day before the settlement date is in the current coupon period. The buyer does not receive the coupon following the trade date but receives the one after that. Accrued interest is minus the interest that would accrue between the value date and the next coupon date.

Example

Suppose a bond pays an annual coupon on the 1st February. The ex-dividend date will be on the 1st business day after the 15th January; assume that this is the 16th January. The number of days accrued interest is shown below for various trade dates (any holidays are ignored in the example).

Trade Date & Day of Week	Value Date	Days Accrued
13th Jan Mon-Wed	15th Jan	344
13th Jan Thu-Fri	17th Jan	346
14th Jan Mon-Wed	16th Jan	345
14th Jan Thu-Fri	18th Jan	347
15th Jan Mon-Wed	17th Jan	346
15th Jan Thu-Fri	19th Jan	348
16th Jan Mon-Wed	18th Jan	−13
16th Jan Thu-Fri	20th Jan	−11
28th Jan Mon-Wed	30th Jan	−1
28th Jan Thu-Fri	1st Feb	0
29th Jan Mon-Wed	31st Jan	0
29th Jan Thu-Fri	2nd Feb	1
30th Jan Mon-Wed	1st Feb	0
30th Jan Thu-Fri	3rd Feb	2
31st Jan Mon-Wed	2nd Feb	1
31st Jan Thu-Fri	4th Feb	3

Market Yield Calculations

There are a number of yield calculation methods in common use in the German Market:

— The AIBD method (see page 108). This method is used by the Bundesbank and the Frankfurt stock exchanges quote sheets.

— The Braess/Fangmeyer method. This is given in Appendix D. It differs from the AIBD method in that payments received after a fraction of a year are discounted using simple interest. This method is used by the savings banks (Sparkassen).

— The Moosmüller method. This is given in Appendix D. It differs from the AIBD method in that payments received after a fraction of a coupon period are discounted using simple interest. This method is used by the pension funds and the Düsseldorf and Munich stock exchange quote sheets.

Schuldscheindarlehen

Schuldscheindarlehen, or Schuldscheine, are loans documented by a promissory note. The first lender holds the Schuldschein itself; subsequent lenders receive a letter of assignment and a copy of the Schuldschein. There are sometimes restrictions placed on the number of times the Schuldschein may be assigned.

Issuers include the Federal government and its agencies, The Federal states and West Berlin, local agencies, state banks, motgage banks and a few corporations and foreigners. Maturities range from 1 to 15 years.

Coupon Dates

Schuldscheine pay interest annually.

Value and Settlement Dates

The settlement date is negotiated. The value date is the same as the settlement date.

Interest Accrual

Schuldscheine are always purchased net of accrued interest. At a coupon payment date the issuer divides the interest among all the holders in the previous year in proportion to the time the Schuldschein was held. The length of holdings is calculated on a 30E/360 basis.

Market Yield Calculations

Care must be taken when calculating the yield for a Schuldschein to make allowance for the way in which accrued interest is handled. The accrued interest is subtracted from the first coupon payment and the clean price equated to the sum of the discounted future cash flows.

Yield calculation methods are as for domestic German bonds.

JAPANESE MARKET

Money Market Instruments	Yields are quoted on an ACT/360 basis.
Government of Japan Bonds	Government of Japan (GOJ) bonds are usually issued with an original maturity of ten years, although longer maturities are also issued. GOJ bonds are not traded ex-dividend.
Coupon Dates	GOJ bonds pay a semi-annual coupon on the 20th of a month.
Value and Settlement Dates	Settlement is on fixed days, namely the 10th, 20th and last day of each month. The settlement date is the nearest fixed date to the trade date. If this would be a non-business day then settlement takes place on the following business day. The value date is the same as the settlement date.
Interest Accrual	Interest accrues on an ACT/365 basis. For bonds bought at primary issuance, interest accrues from and including the issuance date up to and including the settlement date.
Market Yield Calculations	GOJ bonds are traded on the basis of simple yield-to-maturity rather than price. The calculation of simple yield-to-maturity is described on page 18.
Samurai Bonds	Samurai bonds are yen-denominated bonds issued by foreign borrowers in the domestic Japanese market. They are issued with maturities of five to twenty years.
Coupon Dates	Samurai bonds pay a semi-annual coupon.
Value and Settlement Dates	The settlement date is five business days after the trade date. The value date is the same as the settlement date.
Interest Accrual	Interest accrues on an ACT/365 basis.
Market Yield Calculations	As for GOJ bonds.

SWEDISH MARKET

Current Swedish legislation forbids foreign investors from purchasing Swedish money market instruments and bonds.

Money Market Instruments

Yields (unusually for money market instruments) are quoted on a 30E/360 basis.

Domestic Market

Swedish bonds are not traded ex-dividend.

Coupon Dates

Swedish bonds usually pay an annual coupon.

Value and Settlement Dates

The settlement date is 4 business days after the trade date. The value date is the same as the settlement date.

Interest Accrual

Interest accrues on a 30E/360 basis.

Market Yield Calculations

Quoted yields are calculated using the AIBD method (see page 108).

SWISS MARKET

Money Market Instruments

Yields and discounts are quoted on an ACT/360 basis.

Domestic and Foreign Bonds

Swiss bonds are not traded ex-dividend.

Coupon Dates

Swiss bonds pay an annual coupon.

Value and Settlement Dates

The value and settlement dates are three business days after the trade date.

Interest Accrual

Interest accrues on a 30/360 basis. Whether the buyer receives the next coupon depends on where the *trade* date is in relation to the coupon date. If the trade date is on the coupon date then the buyer does not receive that coupon. If the trade date is before the coupon date then the buyer receives the next coupon. This means that if the trade date is in one coupon period and the settlement date is in the next then the number of days accrued interest is greater than or equal to 360.

Market Yield Calculations

The AIBD method is most commonly used (see page 108).

Credit Suisse in its quoted yield figures uses an approximation to calculate accrued interest. If G is the coupon and K is the fraction of a period from settlement to the next coupon, then the accrued interest is approximated as:

$$G \times \frac{100}{Y_a} \times \left((1 + \frac{Y_a}{100})^{1-K} - 1 \right)$$

where Y_a is the annually compounded yield. For low yields this is close to the exact accrued interest:

$$G \times (1 - K)$$

Even for yields as high as 10% the error in using the approximation is only 1% of a coupon. The advantage in using this approximation is that it simplifies the yield formula.

U.K. MARKET

The U.K. market can be divided into the following sectors:

Money Market Instruments
Gilt-edged Securities ('gilts')
Local Authority, Corporation and Bulldog Bonds
Debentures and Unsecured Loan Stock

Money Market Instruments

Discounts and yields are quoted on an ACT/365 basis.

Gilt-Edged Securities

Gilt-edged securities ('gilts') are any securities guaranteed by the U.K. Government excluding Treasury Bills.

Most gilts are either redeemed on a specific date or must be redeemed at any time between two specified dates.

Convertible gilts can be converted into another gilt on certain dates at the option of investor. The conversion terms worsen the later the conversion takes place (see page 56).

For index-linked stocks the interest payments and the final redemption value are related to the Retail Price Index (see page 52).

Two gilts have sinking funds. For Redemption 3% 1986/96 the sinking fund has the option of buying in outstanding bonds or investing in similar issues. For Conversion 3½% 1961/*after* not less than 1% nominal of the amount outstanding at the end of any half-year in which the daily average price is below 90 is used in the next half-year to retire bonds. For both gilts the effect of the sinking fund is usually ignored when calculating yields.

It is becoming increasingly common for gilts to be issued in partly paid form, the balance being paid in instalments before the first coupon date. The first coupon payment is less than the normal coupon (see page 87).

Coupon Dates

Gilts generally pay interest semi-annually. The exception is Consol 2½% which pays interest quarterly.

Value and Settlement Dates	The value and settlement dates are on the next business day following the trade date.
Interest Accrual	Interest accrues on an ACT/365 basis.
Ex-Dividend Dates	Gilts generally go ex-dividend 37 days before the nominal payment date or, if this would be a non-business day, then on the next business day. The exception to the above rule is for a gilt which has a nominal payment date on the 5th, 6th, 7th or 8th of January, April, July or October. In this case the ex-dividend date is the first of the previous month or, if this would be a non-business day, then on the next business day.

For gilts with more than 5 years to maturity, excepting 3½ % War Loan 1952/*after*, there is a three week period before the nominal ex-dividend date during which the stock can be traded cum-dividend or ex-dividend. During this period two prices are quoted and the gilt is said to trade special ex-dividend. If three weeks before the nominal ex-dividend date is a non-business day then the stock starts trading special ex-dividend on the next business day.

Market Yield Calculations	For gilts with only one coupon payment outstanding, it is common practice to calculate yields using simple interest on an ACT/365 basis. This allows direct comparison with sterling money market instruments.

For gilts with more than one coupon payment outstanding, many different methods are used for calculating yields, all giving slightly different results. A few of the commonly used methods are decribed below.

Consortium Yields
For standard gilts (i.e. neither convertible nor indexed-linked) the yield is calculated using the General Bond Formula of Appendix B with interest accrued on an ACT/365 basis. If the gilt is redeemable, then the minimum of the yield-to-call and the yield-to-maturity is quoted ('yield-to-worst').

For convertible gilts the yield is calculated as for a standard gilt assuming the conversion option is not exercised.

For index-linked gilts the real yield is quoted. The future coupon payments and the redemption amount are estimated using the latest RPI figure and the latest inflation rate. Having estimated the future cash flows the money yield and hence the real yield can be calculated. Appendix C gives the details.

Greenwell Montagu Yields

Yields are calculated allowing for the exact number of days to each payment taking into account holidays and weekends. The formula of Appendix A is used with a 365 day year.

Callable, convertible and index-linked gilts are handled in an analogous fashion to the Consortium method.

Datastream Yields

For gilts with maturities of up to 6 years, yields are calculated allowing for the exact number of days to each payment taking into account holidays and weekends. The formula of Appendix A is used with a 365.25 day year. For maturities greater than 6 years, equal length coupon periods are assumed giving the same results as the Consortium yields.

Callable, convertible and index-linked gilts are handled in an analogous fashion to the Consortium method.

Local Authority, Corporation and Bulldog Bonds

Bulldog bonds are foreign bonds issued in the United Kingdom.

Coupon Dates

Interest is usually paid semi-annually.

Value and Settlement Dates

These bonds are usually traded for settlement on the next business day but a few are traded for settlement on a Stock Exchange account day.

The value date is the same as the settlement date.

Interest Accrual	Interest accrues on a ACT/365 basis.
Ex-Dividend Dates	At some time in a coupon period the borrower informs the Stock Exchange as to when a bond is to be traded ex-dividend. The ex-dividend date is usually about 4 weeks before the coupon date but varies from coupon to coupon and from bond to bond.
	Most of these bonds can be traded special ex-dividend 3 weeks before the announced ex-dividend date.
Market Yield Calculations	As for gilts.
Debentures and Unsecured Loan Stock	Debentures are bonds secured by an asset. Prices are usually quoted dirty, i.e. including accrued interest. However, prices for the most frequently traded debentures are quoted clean.
Coupon Dates	Most debentures and unsecured loan stock pay interest semi-annually, a few quarterly or annually.
Value and Settlement Dates	Debentures and unsecured loan stock are traded for settlement on a Stock Exchange account day. The value date is the same as the settlement date.
Interest Accrual	Interest accrues on an ACT/365 basis.
Ex-Dividend Dates	The borrower informs the Stock Exchange as to the date on which a bond is to trade ex-dividend. Debentures and unsecured loan stock are not generally traded special ex-dividend.
Market Yield Calculations	As for gilts.

U.S. MARKET

The U.S. market can be divided up into the following sectors:

Money Market Instruments
U.S. Treasury Notes and Bonds
Agencies, Corporates and Yankees

Mortgage-backed securities, which form an important part of the U.S. bond market, are not considered here. The calculation of yields for these instruments is complicated by uncertainties in the pattern of pre-payments and is beyond the scope of this document.

U.S. bonds are not traded ex-dividend.

Money Market Instruments

Treasury bills, bankers acceptances and commercial paper are sold on the basis of a discount to par. The rate of discount is quoted on an ACT/360 basis. It is common to convert the rate of discount to an equivalent bond yield (see page 7 for the method of calculation).

The yields on CDs are quoted on an ACT/360 basis.

US Treasury Notes and Bonds

Coupon Dates

Interest is paid semi-annually.

Value and Settlement Dates

The settlement date is most commonly on the business day following the trade date. The value date is the same as the settlement date.

Interest Accrual

Interest accrues on an ACT/ACT basis.

Market Yield Calculations

For notes and bonds in their final coupon period quoted yields are calculated using simple interest on an ACT/ACT basis. See Appendix B.

For notes and bonds with more than one coupon to go quoted yields are calculated using the General Bond Formula of Appendix B with interest accrued on an ACT/ACT basis.

Federal Agencies, Corporates and Yankees

Coupon Dates

For most issues interest is paid semi-annually. Some Corporate bonds pay a quarterly or annual coupon. Some Corporate bonds have sinking funds.

Value and Settlement Dates

For Agencies the settlement date is most commonly on the next business day following the trade date. For Corporates and Yankees settlement is five business days after the trade date.

 The value date is the same as the settlement date.

Interest Accrual

Interest accrues on a 30/360 basis.

Market Yield Calculations

In the final coupon period, quoted yields are calculated using simple interest on a 30/360 basis. See Appendix B.

When there is more than one coupon to go, quoted yields are calculated using the General Bond Formula of Appendix B with interest accrued on a 30/360 basis.

EUROMARKET

Money Market Instruments
The discounts and yields of money market instruments are quoted on an ACT/360 basis.

Eurobonds
A wide variety of structures have been used in the Eurobond market.*

Coupon Dates
Most Eurobonds pay interest annually although a few pay semi-annually.

Value and Settlement Dates
The value date is 7 days after the trade date. Normally the settlement date is the same as the value date. However, if the value date coincides with a bank holiday in the centre where the payment and/or delivery is to be effected then the settlement date will be on the first business day following the bank holiday in that centre.

Interest Accrual
Interest accrues on a 30E/360 basis. This is in accordance with Rules 224 and 225 of the AIBD statutes, modified on 21st March, 1986 and which come into effect on 1st January, 1987. The original versions of these rules did not make it clear how the case should be handled where the previous coupon date and/or the value date is the 31st of a month.

Ex-Dividend Dates
Eurobonds are not generally traded ex-dividend.

However, in the Euro Deutsche Mark market bonds are traded ex-dividend. The rules for determining the ex-dividend date are the same as for the domestic Deutsche Mark market allowing for the fact that settlement is usually 7 days after the trade date.

---

*For details of the wide variety of structures that have been used in the Euromarket see 'Innovation in the structures of international securities', CSFB Research, 1986.

Market Yield Calculations Quoted yields are calculated using the AIBD method. This is equivalent to using the General Bond Formula of Appendix B with interest accrued on a 30E/360 basis. For bonds with a sinking fund the yield-to-average-life rather than the yield-to-equivalent-life is quoted. Annually compounded yields are always quoted.

The AIBD method is not as precisely defined as is commonly thought. The uncertainty lies with the calculation of yields for bonds in their final coupon period.

The AIBD 'Yield Book' gives a formula for calculating yields which is applicable to bonds in their final coupon period. This gives a yield assuming daily compounding of interest over fractional coupon periods. The 'Yield Book' gives tables showing the yields for a range of prices, maturities and coupons. However, since yields for maturities less than one year are not quoted, one cannot be certain as to how bonds in their final coupon period should be handled.

The AIBD 'Weekly Eurobond Guide' calculates yields for most bonds in their final coupon period assuming daily compounding of interest. However, for a few bonds it calculates yields using simple interest based on actual days in a 365 day year. Why this is done only for a few bonds and why a 365 day year is used (360 days would allow comparison with Euro money market instruments) is far from clear.

It is a common belief in the markets that the AIBD method assumes daily compounding of interest for bonds of any maturity. This is the assumption made in this publication.

Appendix A: Consistent Yield Formula

Introduction

A consistent method for calculating yields considers the exact days on which future cash flows occur and discounts them using the same interest rate. The sum of the discounted cash flows is equated to the price paid for the bond.

Suppose a bond provides cash flows CF_i, D_i days after settlement. The yield, Y_h, compounded H times per annum and based on a year of A_y days can be derived from:

$$\text{Dirty Price} = \text{Clean Price} + \text{Accrued} = \sum_i \frac{CF_i}{\left(1 + \dfrac{Y_h}{H \times 100}\right)^{\frac{D_i \times H}{A_y}}}$$

Obvious choices for A_y are 360, 365 or 365.25 according to taste. H will often be the same as the number of coupon payments per annum. It is straightforward to convert between yields calculated with different values of A_y and H. If Y_h is the yield calculated on the basis (H, A_y), and Y_h' is the yield calculated on the basis (H′, A_y') then the relationship between them is:

$$\left(1 + \frac{Y_h}{H \times 100}\right)^{H/A_y} = \left(1 + \frac{Y_h'}{H' \times 100}\right)^{H'/A_y'}$$

After the initial payment for the bond the following cash flows need to be taken into consideration:

— Any further payments for partially paid bonds.

— Coupon payments.

— Redemption payments. Some bonds have a redemption schedule or sinking fund which redeems a certain percentage of the issue at each coupon payment. Such a bond can be regarded as a portfolio of bullet bonds with maturities equal to the coupon dates. The proportion in the portfolio of the bond maturing on the ith coupon date is given by the proportion of the total issue redeemed on that date.

— Tax payments when calculating net yields. In the formulae given below it is assumed that coupon payments are liable for income tax and redemption payments are liable for capital gains tax. Furthermore it is assumed that tax is paid at the time payment is received; this is unlikely to be the case in practice.

Before giving the formula which relates yield to price the notation using in the appendices is explained.

Notation

P_c = clean price, i.e. the price excluding accrued interest, per 100 units face value.

P_d = dirty price, i.e. the price including accrued interest, per 100 units face value.

I_1 = interest accrued at the time of purchase.

I_r = interest accrued at the time of the final redemption date. This is zero if the redemption date is the same as the final coupon date.

H = number of coupon payments per annum.

A_y = number of days in a year

Y_h = yield compounded H times per annum %.

Y_a = annually compounded yield %.

N = number of coupon payments still to be made.

D_i = number of days from settlement to coupon payment i.

D_r = number of days from settlement to the final redemption payment.

G_i = the ith coupon rate expressed as a percentage of the face value *per annum*. The actual coupon payment received is:

$$\frac{G_i}{H}$$

Frequently coupon payments are constant, i.e. $G_i = G$ for all i.

The most common exceptions to this are:

a) Stepped coupons. Successive coupon payments change according to a schedule determined at the time of issue.

111

b) Indexed coupons. The coupon payments
    are related to some index, e.g. Retail
    Price Index or cost of oil. In order to
    calculate a yield some assumption has to
    be made about the future values of the
    index.

c) Bonds traded ex-dividend. In this case
    $G_1 = 0$ but subsequent coupons are
    constant.

d) The next coupon is the first since issue
    and it makes a non-standard payment.
    This is particularly common for bonds
    issued on a partially paid basis.

X_i = rate of income tax/100. When calculating
gross yields this should be set to zero.

X_c = rate of capital gains tax/100. When
calculating gross yields this should be set to
zero.

G_i' = the ith coupon payment net of tax. The way
this is calculated varies from market to
market. Most commonly it is related to the
coupon rate G_i by:

$$G_i' = \underline{G_i} \times (1 - X_i)$$
$$H$$

However, it is possible that the first coupon
payment might be taxed differently from
subsequent payments. For example, if the
first payment is taxed only on the interest
accrued since purchase:

$$G_1 = \underline{G_1} \times (1 - X_i) + I_1 \times X_i$$
$$H$$

Other variations also occur.

L = number of part payments still to be made
($= 0$ if fully paid).

A_j = part payments, $j = 1, ..., L$

M_j = number of days between settlement and part
payment j.

S_i = fraction of the currently outstanding issue redeemed by the redemption schedule at the time of the ith coupon payment.

S_r = fraction of the currently outstanding issue redeemed at the the final redemption date. Clearly:

$$S_r = 1 - \sum_{i=1}^{N} S_i$$

R_i = redemption payment when redeemed by the redemption schedule at the time of the ith coupon payment.

R_r = final redemption payment.

Yield Formula

The formula relating dirty price to yield is:

$$P_d \times (1 - X_c \times (S_r \times V^{T_r} + [\sum_{i=1}^{N} S_i \times V^{T_i}])) + \sum_{j=1}^{L} A_j \times V^{E_j}$$

$$= \sum_{i=1}^{N} G_i' \times V^{T_i} + R_r' \times S_r \times V^{T_r} +$$

$$[\sum_{i=1}^{N} V^{T_i} \times (S_i \times R_i' - G_i' \times \sum_{j=1}^{i-1} S_j)] \qquad (A1)$$

where:

$$V = \frac{1}{\left(1 + \dfrac{Y_h}{100 \times H}\right)}$$

$$E_j = \frac{M_j \times H}{A_y}$$

$$T_i = \frac{D_i \times H}{A_y}$$

$$T_r = \frac{D_r \times H}{A_y}$$

P_t = sum of all remaining part payments ie:

$$P_t = \sum_{j=1}^{L} A_j$$

$$R_i' = R_i - (R_i - P_t\{+I_1\}) \times X_c$$

$$R_r' = R_r - (R_r - P_t\{+I_1\}) \times X_c + I_r \times (1 - X_i)$$

The terms in curly brackets in the formula for R_i' and R_r' should be omitted if capital gains tax is paid on the difference between the dirty price and the redemption payment. They should be retained if capital gains tax is paid on the difference between the clean price and the redemption payment. If a capital loss is not allowable as a tax credit, X_c should be set to zero for bonds trading above par.

All terms in square brackets can be ignored if the bond does not have a redemption schedule; in such a case $S_r = 1$.

This formula can be solved for Y_h given P_d using the Newton-Raphson method. The first derivative of P_d with respect to Y_h can be derived from:

$$\frac{dP_d}{dY_h} = \frac{-V^2}{H \times 100} \times \frac{dP_d}{dV} \qquad (A2)$$

where:

$$V \times \frac{dP_d}{dV} \times (1 - X_c \times (S_r \times V^{T_r} + [\sum_{i=1}^{N} S_i \times V^{T_i}])) -$$

$$P_d \times X_c \times (S_r \times T_r \times V^{T_r} + [\sum_{i=1}^{N} T_i \times S_i \times V^{T_i}]) +$$

$$\sum_{j=1}^{L} A_j \times E_j \times V^{E_j} =$$

$$\sum_{i=1}^{N} G'_i \times T_i \times V^{T_i} + R'_r \times T_r \times S_r \times V^{T_r} +$$

$$[\sum_{i=1}^{N} T_i \times V^{T_i} \times (S'_i \times R'_i - G'_i \times \sum_{j=1}^{i-1} S_j)]$$

Solving for the Yield

To find the yield corresponding to a given price, P'_d, the Newton-Raphson method is used as follows. Suppose $Y_h[k]$ is the kth approximation and that the corresponding price and derivative calculated using formulae A1 and A2 are $P_d(Y_h[k])$ and $\dfrac{dP_d}{dY_h}\Big|_{Y_h = Y_h[k]}$ respectively.

A better approximation, $Y_h[k+1]$, is given by:

$$Y_h[k+1] = Y_h[k] + \frac{P'_d - P_d(Y_h[k])}{\dfrac{dP_d}{dY_h}\Big|_{Y_h = Y_h[k]}}$$

As a starting approximation take:

$$Y_h[0] = \frac{\bar{G} \times 100 \times (1 - X_i)}{P_c}$$

where $\bar{G}$ is a typical coupon rate, e.g. the average of the G_i. (More sophisticated initial approximations can be used but since the method converges quickly they provide little additional benefit.) Iterate until:

$$\frac{|P'_d - P_d(Y_h[k])|}{P'_d} < e$$

where e is the acceptable level of error (10^{-6} should be sufficiently accurate for most purposes).

Example
Suppose the U.K. gilt-edged security Exchequer 2.5% maturing on 24th February, 1987 is traded for settlement on 3rd July, 1986 at a clean price of $96^{13}/_{16}$. The bond pays a semi-annual coupon. What is its gross yield?

First the accrued interest must be calculated. In the U.K. domestic market interest accrues on an ACT/365 basis. The last coupon payment was on 24th February, 1986 so there are 129 days accrued interest. Therefore the dirty price of the bond is given by:

$$P'_d = 96 + \frac{13}{16} + \frac{129}{365} \times 2.5 = 97.6961$$

To calculate the yield on the basis of a 365 day year, take $A_y = 365$. There are two coupon payments outstanding. The first payment is nominally on 24th August, 1986. This is, however, a Sunday. The 25th August, 1986 happens to be a public holiday so payment will actually take place on 26th August, 1986, 54 days after settlement. Therefore:

$$D_1 = 54 \quad T_1 = \frac{54 \times 2}{365} = 0.2959$$

$$G_1 = 2.5 \quad G'_1 = \frac{2.5}{2} = 1.25$$

The final payment is nominally on 24th February, 1987, 236 days after settlement. This date is not on a weekend or a public holiday so payment will take place on this date. Therefore:

$$D_2 = 236 \quad T_2 = \frac{236 \times 2}{365} = 1.2932$$

$$G_2 = 2.5 \quad G'_2 = \frac{2.5}{2} = 1.25$$

The bond does not have a sinking fund and the last redemption payment takes place at the time of the final coupon payment. Therefore:

$$S_1 = 0 \quad S_2 = 0 \quad S_r = 1$$

$$T_r = T_2 = 1.2932$$

$$R'_r = R_r = 100$$

There are no outstanding part payments. Since we are calculating the gross yield $X_c = X_i = 0$. Substituting in formulae A1 and A2 gives the equations:

$$P_d = 1.25 \times V^{0.2959} + 1.25 \times V^{1.2932} + 100 \times V^{1.2932}$$

$$\frac{dP_d}{dY_h} = \frac{-V^2}{H \times 100} \times \frac{dP_d}{dV}$$

$$V \times \frac{dP_d}{dV} = 1.25 \times 0.2959 \times V^{0.2959} +$$

$$1.25 \times 1.2932 \times V^{1.2932} + 100 \times 1.2932 \times V^{1.2932}$$

The initial approximation for Y_h is given by:

$$Y_h[0] = \frac{\bar{G} \times 100}{P_c} = \frac{2.5 \times 100}{96 + \dfrac{13}{16}} = 2.582 \quad V[0] = 0.9873$$

This gives:

$$P_d(Y_h[0]) = 100.8294$$

$$\frac{dP_d}{dY_h}\bigg|_{Y_h = Y_h[0]} = -0.6375$$

The Newton-Raphson method gives for the next approximation:

$$Y_h[1] = 2.582 + \frac{97.6961 - 100.8294}{-0.6375} = 7.4974$$

Subsequent iterations give:

$$Y_h[1] = 7.4974 \quad V[1] = 0.9639 \quad P_d(Y_h[1]) = 97.7809$$

$$\frac{dP_d}{dV}\bigg|_{Y_h = Y_h[1]} = 129.906 \qquad \frac{dP_d}{dY_h}\bigg|_{Y_h = Y_h[1]} = -0.6034$$

$$Y_h[1] = 7.6379 \quad V[2] = 0.9632 \quad P_d(Y_h[2]) = 97.6961$$

$$\frac{dP_d}{dV}\bigg|_{Y_h = Y_h[2]} = 129.881 \qquad \frac{dP_d}{dY_h}\bigg|_{Y_h = Y_h[2]} = -0.6025$$

$$Y_h[3] = 7.6380 \quad V[3] = 0.9632 \quad P_d(Y_h[3]) = 97.6961$$

$$\frac{dP_d}{dV}\bigg|_{Y_h = Y_h[3]} = 129.881 \qquad \frac{dP_d}{dY_h}\bigg|_{Y_h = Y_h[3]} = -0.6025$$

After three iterations the price calculated from the approximate yield equals the actual price to four decimal places. Therefore the yield is 7.638%.

Annually Compounded Yield

The annually compounded yield, Y_a, can easily be derived from the yield compounded every $1/H$ years, Y_h from the formula:

$$Y_a = \left(\left(1 + \frac{Y_h}{100 \times H}\right)^H - 1\right) \times 100 \qquad \text{(A3)}$$

Average Life

The average life in years, AL, is given by:

$$AL = \frac{1}{H} \times \frac{\displaystyle\sum_{i=1}^{N} S_i \times R_i \times T_i + S_r \times R_r \times T_r}{\displaystyle\sum_{i=1}^{N} S_i \times R_i + S_r \times R_r} \qquad \text{(A4)}$$

Equivalent Life

The equivalent life in years, EL, is given by:

$$EL = \frac{1}{H} \times \frac{\displaystyle\sum_{i=1}^{N} S_i \times R_i \times T_i \times V^{T_i} + S_r \times R_r \times T_r \times V^{T_r}}{\displaystyle\sum_{i=1}^{N} S_i \times R_i \times V^{T_r} + S_r \times R_r \times V^{T_r}} \qquad \text{(A5)}$$

Duration

The duration, D, in years is given by:

$$D = \frac{V}{H} \times \frac{1}{P_d} \times \frac{dP_d}{dV} \times (1 - X_c \times (S_r \times V^{T_r} + [\sum_{i=1}^{N} S_i \times V^{T_i}])) \qquad \text{(A6)}$$

Example
For the U.K. gilt-edged security Exchequer 2.5% maturing 24th February, 1987 it was found that:

$$V = 0.9632 \quad \frac{dP_d}{dV} = 129.881 \quad P_d = 97.6961$$

Therefore:

$$D = \frac{0.9632}{2} \times \frac{1}{97.6961} \times 129.881 = 0.640 \text{ years}$$

Modified Duration and Volatility

Modified duration or volatility is defined as:

$$MD = -\frac{100}{P_d} \times \frac{dP_d}{dY_h} = \frac{V^2}{H} \times \frac{dP_d}{dV} \qquad \text{(A7)}$$

Note that the commonly stated relationship between modified duration and duration—

$$MD = \frac{D}{\left(1 + \frac{Y_h}{H \times 100}\right)}$$

only holds in the case when the rate of capital gains tax, X_c, is zero. (In practice, duration and modified duration are nearly always calculated for gross cash flows.)

Convexity

Convexity, Cx, is defined as:

$$Cx = \frac{10000}{P_d} \times \frac{d^2P_d}{dY_h^2}$$

or in terms of derivatives with respect to V:

$$Cx = \frac{V^2}{H^2} \times \frac{1}{P_d} \times \left(V^2 \times \frac{d^2P_d}{dV^2} + 2 \times V \times \frac{dP_d}{dV}\right) \qquad \text{(A8)}$$

The second derivative of P_d with respect to V can be derived from:

$$\frac{V^2 \times d^2P_d}{dV^2} \times \left(1 - X_c \times \left(S_r \times V^{T_r} + \left[\sum_{i=1}^{N} S_i \times V^{T_i}\right]\right)\right)$$

$$-2 \times V \times \frac{dP_d}{dV} \times X_c \times \left(S_r \times T_r \times V^{T_r} + \left[\sum_{i=1}^{N} S_i \times T_i \times V^{T_i}\right]\right) -$$

$$P_d \times X_c \times (S_r \times T_r \times (T_r - 1) \times V^{T_r})$$

$$+ \left[\sum_{i=1}^{N} T_i \times (T_i - 1) \times S_i \times V^{T_i}\right] +$$

$$\sum_{j=1}^{L} A_j \times E_j \times (E_j - 1) \times V^{E_j} =$$

$$\sum_{i=1}^{N} G'_i \times T_i \times (T_i - 1) \times V^{T_i} + R'_r \times T_r \times (T_r - 1) \times V^{T_r} +$$

$$[\sum_{i=1}^{N} T_i \times (T_i - 1) \times V^{T_i} \times (S_i \times R'_i - G'_i \times \sum_{j=1}^{i-1} S_j)] \quad (A9)$$

Example

Continuing the example of the U.K. gilt-edged security, Exchequer 2.5%, substituting in A9 gives:

$$V^2 \times \frac{d^2 P_d}{dV^2} = 1.25 \times 0.2959 \times (0.2959 - 1) \times V^{0.2959}$$

$$+ 1.25 \times 1.2932 \times (1.2932 - 1) \times V^{1.2932}$$

$$+ 100 \times 1.2932 \times (1.2932 - 1) \times V^{1.2932}$$

$$= 36.3092$$

Substituting in A8 gives the convexity:

$$Cx = \frac{0.9632^2}{2^2} \times \frac{1}{97.6961} \times (36.3092 + 2 \times 0.9632 \times 129.881)$$

$$= 0.68$$

Rather than using a cumbersome formula like A9 it is often easier to use the following approximation. Let the prices calculated for a one basis point increase and decrease of the yield be P_p and P_m respectively. The convexity is given approximately by:

$$Cx = \left(\frac{P_p + P_m - 2 \times P_d}{P_d}\right) \times 10^8$$

For the example: $P_d = 97.69606$

$$P_p = 97.69003$$

$$P_m = 97.70208$$

$$Cx = \left(\frac{97.69003 + 97.70208 - 2 \times 97.69606}{97.69606}\right) \times 10^8 = 0.68$$

which agrees with the result calculated previously.

Appendix B: Market Yield Calculations

The method given in Appendix A for the calculation of bond yields, although logically consistent, is not commonly used in the bond markets. The most significant deviations from the method of Appendix A that can occur are:

1) For bonds in their last coupon period a simple interest formula is sometimes used.

2) No allowance is made for the fact that a nominal coupon or redemption payment date might fall on a non-business day.

3) Periods between coupons are assumed to be of equal length.

4) Fractional coupon periods are calculated on the same basis as accrued interest.

If the periods between coupons are assumed to be of equal length then the following approximation can be made:

$$T_i = K_1 + i - 1$$
$$T_r = K_1 + N - 1 + K_r \tag{B1}$$

In other words the number of periods to a coupon payment consists of a fractional part, K_1, plus a whole number of coupon periods. The redemption payment occurs a fraction of a period, K_r, after the last coupon payment.

It is often the case that the fractions of a period, K_1 and K_r, are calculated on the basis that is implied by the method used for calculating accrued interest in the particular market.

For example, in the U.S. Treasury market interest is accrued on an ACT/ACT basis. Suppose the next coupon date for a U.S. Treasury is 15th September, 1986 and the settlement date is 2nd August, 1986. The number of days in the current coupon period is 184. The number of days from settlement to the next coupon is 44. Therefore K_1, the fraction of a period from settlement to the next coupon, is:

$$K_1 = \frac{44}{184} = 0.239$$

For gilt-edged securities interest is accrued on an ACT/365 basis. Thus for a semi-annual coupon the length of a standard coupon period is 182.5 days. For a gilt with the same settlement and payment dates as the U.S. Treasury, K_1 is given by:

$$K_1 = \frac{44}{182.5} = 0.241$$

In all the formulae quoted below it is assumed that K_1 and K_r are calculated on the same basis as accrued interest in the particular market.

For partly paid bonds the fractions of a period to the future installments, E_j, should also be calculated on the same basis as accrued interest in the particular market.

The advantage of making the approximations (B1) is that if a series of coupon payments is the same, then a closed form for the sum of their present values can be found. It is assumed in the following formulae that the first coupon payment is possibly non-standard and is equivalent to an annual rate of $G_1\%$. All subsequent payments are the same and equivalent to an annual rate of $G\%$.

Formula (A1) under these assumptions becomes:

General Bond Formula

$$P_d \times (1 - X_c \times (S_r \times V^{T_r} + [\sum_{i=1}^{N} S_i \times V^{T_i}])) +$$

$$\sum_{j=1}^{L} A_j \times V^{E_j} =$$

$$R_r' \times S_r \times V^{T_r} + V^{K_1} \times \left(G_1' + G' \times \frac{(V - V^N)}{1 - V} \right) +$$

$$[\sum_{i=1}^{N} V^{T_i} \times (S_i \times R_i' - G_i' \times \sum_{j=1}^{i-1} S_j)] \tag{B2}$$

This formula is widely used to calculate quoted bond yields. It is used to calculate the following quoted yields:

— U.S. Treasuries with more than one coupon to maturity;

— U.S. Federal Agencies, Corporates and Yankees with more than one coupon to maturity;

— Yields calculated according to the AIBD method;

— The Consortium yields for U.K. gilt-edged securities with more than one coupon to maturity.

However, for bonds in their last coupon period a simple interest formula is sometimes used (see page 129).

The first derivative of P_d with respect to V is needed to solve B2 iteratively using the Newton-Raphson method:

$$V \times \frac{dP_d}{dV} \times (1 - X_c \times (S_r \times V^{T_r} + [\sum_{i=1}^{N} S_i \times V^{T_i}])) -$$

$$P_d \times X_c \times (S_r \times T_r \times V^{T_r} + [\sum_{i=1}^{N} T_i \times S_i \times V^{T_i}]) +$$

$$\sum_{j=1}^{L} A_j \times E_j \times V^{E_j} =$$

$$R_r' \times T_r \times S_r \times V^{T_r} + G_i' \times K_1 \times V^{K_1} +$$

$$G' \times \frac{V^{K_1}}{(1-V)^2} \times (V^{N+1} \times [N-1+K_1] - V^N \times [N+K_1] -$$

$$K_1 \times V^2 + V \times [1+K_1]) +$$

$$[\sum_{i=1}^{N} T_i \times V^{T_i} \times (S_i \times R_i' - G_i' \times \sum_{j=1}^{i-1} S_j)] \qquad \text{(B3)}$$

Formulae B2 and B3 simplify considerably under certain assumptions about the cash flow patterns. Some important cases are given below.

No Redemption Schedule If there is no redemption schedule then:

$$S_i = 0 \quad i = 1 \ldots N$$
$$S_r = 1$$

Substituting in B2 and B3 gives:

$$P_d \times (1 - X_c \times V^{T_r}) + \sum_{j=1}^{L} A_j \times V^{E_j} = R_r' \times V^{T_r} +$$
$$V^{K_1} \times \left(G_i' + G' \times \frac{(V - N)}{1 - V} \right) \tag{B4}$$

$$V \times \frac{dP_d}{dV} \times (1 - X_c \times V^{T_r}) -$$

$$P_d \times X_c \times T_r \times V^{T_r} + \sum_{j=1}^{L} A_j \times E_j \times V^{E_j} =$$
$$R_r' \times T_r \times V^{T_r} + G_i' \times K_1 \times V^{K_1} + \tag{B5}$$
$$G' \times \frac{V^{K_1}}{(1-V)^2} \times (V^{N+1} \times [N - 1 + K_1] - V^N \times [N + K_1] -$$
$$K_1 \times V^2 + V \times [1 + K_1])$$

Perpetual For an irredeemable bond letting N and T_r tend to infinity in B4 and B5 gives:

$$P_d + \sum_{j=1}^{L} A_j \times V^{E_j} = V^{K_1} \times \left(G_i' + G' \times \frac{V}{(1 - V)} \right) \tag{B6}$$

$$V \times \frac{dP_d}{dV} + \sum_{j=1}^{L} A_j \times E_j \times V^{E_j} = \tag{B7}$$

$$G_i' \times K_1 \times V^{K_1} + G' \times \frac{V^{K_1}}{(1-V)^2} \times ((1 + K_1) \times V - K_1 \times V^2)$$

Uniform Redemption Schedule

Most commonly, sinking funds redeem an issue in equal proportions from some start date up to maturity. In this case, B2 simplifies considerably with the following assumptions:

a) Final redemption date equals last full coupon date:

$$S_r = 0$$

b) Uniform redemption schedule, active over W coupon periods, all redemptions at the same price:

$$S_i = 0 \qquad i = 1,...,N-W$$

$$S_i = \frac{1}{W} \qquad i = N-W+1,...,N$$

$$R_i' = R' \qquad i = N-W+1,...,N$$

c) No part payments outstanding:

$$L = 0$$

d) All coupon payments equal:

$$G_i' = G'$$

Substituting in B2 and B3 gives:

$$P_d \times (1 - X_c \times Z) = \frac{V^{K_1}}{(1-V)} \times \tag{B8}$$

$$\left(G' + \frac{V^{N-W}}{W} \times (R' \times (1-V^W) + G' \times \frac{(V^{W+1}-V)}{1-V}) \right)$$

$$V \times \frac{dP_d}{dV} \times (1 - X_c \times Z) -$$

$$X_c \times P_d \times Z \times \left(K_1 + N-W + \frac{V}{1-V} - \frac{W \times V^W}{1-V^W} \right) =$$

$$\left(K_1 + \frac{V}{1-V} \right) \times P_d \times (1 - X_c \times Z) +$$

$$\frac{V^{K_1+N}}{1-V} \times \frac{1}{W} \times \{R' \times ((N\text{-}W) \times V^{-W} - N) + \qquad \text{(B9)}$$

$$\frac{G'}{(1-V)^2} \times V \times$$

$$[N+1-(N\text{-}W+1) \times V^{-W} - N \times V + (N\text{-}W) \times V^{-W+1}]\}$$

where:

$$Z = \frac{V^{K_1+N-W}}{W} \times \frac{(1-V^W)}{1-V}$$

Example

The U.S. Treasury bond 11.75% maturing on 15th February, 2001 is traded for settlement on 4th September, 1986 at a price of $134^{22}/_{32}$. What is the quoted gross yield?

For a U.S. Treasury with more than one coupon to maturity, quoted yields are calculated using the General Bond Formula.

Accrued interest is calculated on an ACT/ACT basis. The previous coupon was on 15th August, 1986, the next coupon on 15th February, 1987. The number of days in the current coupon period is 184. The number of days from the previous coupon to settlement is 20. Therefore the dirty price is:

$$P'_d = 134 + \frac{22}{32} + \frac{20}{2 \times 184} \times 11.75 = 135.326$$

The bond pays a semi-annual coupon ($H = 2$) and the number of coupon payments remaining, N, is 29. All coupon payments are the same, there is no redemption schedule and the bond is redeemed on the last coupon date. Therefore the simplified formulae B4 and B5 can be used with:

$$G_1 = G = 11.75$$

$$G'_1 = G' = \frac{11.75}{2} = 5.875$$

$$R'_r = 100$$

The number of days from settlement to the next coupon is 164, so:

$$K_1 = \frac{164}{184} = 0.8913$$

Therefore, since there are no part payments:

$$P_d = V^{0.8913} \times \left(5.875 + 5.875 \times \frac{(V - V^{29})}{1 - V} + 100 \times V^{29-1}\right)$$

$$V \times \frac{dP_d}{dV} = 100 \times (29-1+0.8913) \times V^{(29-1+0.8913)} +$$

$$5.875 \times 0.8913 \times V^{0.8913} + 5.875 \times$$

$$\frac{V^{0.8913}}{(1-V)^2} \times [(29-1+0.8913) \times V^{29+1} - (29+0.8913) \times V^{29} -$$

$$0.8913 \times V^2 + V \times (1+0.8913)]$$

The yield can be found using the Newton-Raphson method as described in Appendix A. The first approximation is given by:

$$Y_h[0] = \frac{11.75}{134.6875} \times 100 = 8.7239$$

Successive iterations give:

$$Y_h[1] = 7.6641 \quad P_d(Y_h[1]) = 135.952$$

$$Y_h[2] = 7.7223 \quad P_d(Y_h[2]) = 135.328$$

$$Y_h[3] = 7.7225 \quad P_d(Y_h[3]) = 135.326$$

After three iterations, the price calculated from the approximate yield equals the actual price to three decimal places. Therefore, the yield is 7.723%.

Example
The Dutch Government bond 10.5% Nederland 1982 maturing on 1st May, 1992 is traded for settlement on 5th September, 1986 at a clean price of 115. The bond pays an annual coupon and has a uniform redemption schedule starting in 1988. What is the gross yield-to-equivalent-life?

First, the accrued interest must be calculated. In the Dutch market interest accrues on a 30E/360 basis, and the value date is the same as the settlement date. There are 124 days from the previous coupon to the value date calculated on a '30E' basis. Therefore:

$$P_d = 115 + \frac{124}{360} \times 10.5 = 118.6167$$

Yields quoted in the Amro Bond Guide are calculated using the AIBD method. There are 236 days from settlement to the next coupon calculated on a '30E' basis. Therefore:

$$K_1 = \frac{236}{360} = 0.6556$$

Since there is a uniform redemption schedule and all coupon payments are the same, formulae B8 and B9 can be used. There are 6 coupon payments outstanding and the redemption schedule is active for 5 years. Therefore:

$$W = 5 \qquad\qquad N = 6$$
$$G' = 10.5 \qquad\qquad R' = 100$$

Since gross yield-to-equivalent-life is being calculated, $X_c = X_i = 0$. Substituing in B8 and B9 gives:

$$P_d = \frac{V^{0.6556}}{1-V} \times \left(10.5 + \frac{V}{5} \times (100 \times (1-V^5) + 10.5 \times \frac{(V^{5+1} - V)}{1-V}\right)$$

$$V \times \frac{dP_d}{dV} = \left(0.6556 + \frac{V}{1-V}\right) \times P_d + \frac{V^{0.6556+6}}{1-V} \times \frac{1}{5} \times$$

$$(100 \times ((6\text{-}5) \times V^{-5} - 6) + \frac{10.5}{(1-V)^2} \times V \times$$

$$[6 + 1 - (6\text{-}5 + 1) \times V^{-5} - 6 \times V + (6\text{-}5) \times V^{-5+1}])$$

The yield can be found using the Newton-Raphson method as described in Appendix A. The first approximation is given by:

$$Y_h[0] = \frac{10.5}{115} \times 100 = 9.1304$$

Succesive iterations give:

$$Y_h[1] = 5.1433 \qquad P_d(Y_h[1]) = 120.786$$
$$Y_h[2] = 5.7702 \qquad P_d(Y_h[2]) = 118.538$$
$$Y_h[3] = 5.7467 \qquad P_d(Y_h[3]) = 118.621$$
$$Y_h[4] = 5.7480 \qquad P_d(Y_h[4]) = 118.616$$

After four iterations, the price has converged sufficiently. Therefore the yield-to-equivalent-life is 5.748%.

Simple Interest Formula for Bonds in their Final Coupon Period

If there is only one payment outstanding then it is not uncommon for a simple interest yield to be calculated with the intention of allowing direct comparison with money market instruments. Logically, in order to allow this comparison to be made, the yield should be calculated exactly the same way as for a Certificate of Deposit in the particular market, i.e. using actual days in a 360 or 365 day year as appropriate. In practice, a simple interest yield is calculated using the same calendar as implied by the accrued interest calculation. Thus, taking $K_r = 0$, the simple interest yield is given by:

$$Y = \left(\frac{(G_1' + R_r) - 1}{P_d} \right) \times \frac{100 \times H}{K_1}$$

Example
The U.S. Treasury bond 6.125% maturing on 15th November, 1986 is traded for settlement on 4th September, 1986 at a clean price of $100 \frac{4}{32}$. In the U.S. market, for bonds in their final coupon period a simple interest formula is used.

Interest accrues on an ACT/ACT basis. The last coupon date was on 15th May, 1986. The number of days in the current coupon period is 184. The number of days from the previous coupon to settlement is 112. Therefore the dirty price is:

$$P_d = 100 + \frac{4}{32} + \frac{112}{2 \times 184} \times 6.125 = 101.989$$

The number of days to maturity is 72. Therefore:

$$K_1 = \frac{72}{184} = 0.3913$$

When calculating the gross yield:

$$G_1' = \frac{6.125}{2} = 3.0625$$

$$R_r' = 100$$

so:

$$Y = \left(\frac{3.0625 + 100 - 1}{101.989}\right) \times \frac{100}{0.3913} \times 2 = 5.38\%$$

Appendix C: Indexed-Linked Gilts

Let the current rate of inflation compounded annually be $J\%$. The relationship between the nominal yield, Y_h, and the real yield, R_h is:

$$1 + \frac{Y_h}{100 \times H} = \left(1 + \frac{R_h}{100 \times H}\right) \times \left(1 + \frac{J}{100}\right)^{1/H}$$

where, as is usual for gilts, $H = 2$. Let the base and current Retail Price Index be RPI_b and RPI_c respectively. The nominal yield, and hence the real yield, can be calculated from formula A1 of Appendix A with the following values for the coupons:

$G_1 =$ the known next coupon payment times 2

$$G_i = G_b \times \frac{RPI_c}{RPI_b} \times \left(1 + \frac{J}{100}\right)^{((i-2)/2 + (M_n - 2)/12)}$$

for $i = 2, \ldots, N$

where M_n is the number of months from the month of the current RPI figure to the month of the next coupon. G_b is the basic coupon rate. The redemption amount, R_r is given by:

$$R_r = 100 \times \frac{RPI_c}{RPI_b} \times \left(1 + \frac{J}{100}\right)^{((N-2)/2 + (M_n - 2)/12)}$$

For an index-linked gilt in its final coupon period all the cash flows are known exactly. In this case, its nominal yield can be calculated as for a straight gilt.

Appendix D: Braess/Fangmeyer and Moosmüller Formulae

The Braess/Fangmeyer and Moosmüller methods differ from the General Bond Formula of Appendix B in the way in which fractional coupon periods are discounted.

The basic idea behind the Braess/Fangmeyer method is as follows. Suppose an account pays/charges a certain rate of interest which is compounded annually. For periods of less than a year simple interest is calculated. Suppose the cash flows from the bond are paid into or withdrawn from the account, and interest is credited to or debited from the account on a fixed day in the year corresponding to the maturity date. The yield according to the Braess/Fangmeyer method is the rate of interest that would have to be paid/charged to leave zero balance when the bond matures.

To see how the Braess/Fangmeyer method works consider a 10% semi-annual coupon bond with 1.75 years to maturity. Suppose the yield according to the Braess/Fangmeyer method is 8%, what would be the dirty price, P_d? The cash flows are shown below:

```
 -P_d     5              5              5            105
  | -------|--------------|--------------|--------------|
 1.75    1.5            1.0            0.5            0.0   Years to
                                                           Maturity
```

The negative cash flow corresponding to the initial payment is charged simple interest for ¾ of a year which is then compounded for one year giving at maturity:

$$-P_d \times \left(1 + 0.75 \times \frac{8}{100}\right) \times \left(1 + \frac{8}{100}\right)$$

The first coupon payment earns simple interest for ½ year which is then compounded for one year giving:

$$5 \times \left(1 + 0.5 \times \frac{8}{100}\right) \times \left(1 + \frac{8}{100}\right)$$

The second coupon payment earns interest for one year giving:

$$5 \times \left(1 + \frac{8}{100}\right)$$

The third coupon payment earns interest for ½ year giving:

$$5 \times \left(1 + 0.5 \times \frac{8}{100}\right)$$

At maturity there is a payment of 105 into the account corresponding to the redemption payment and the final coupon.

All these amounts left in the account at maturity must sum to zero, giving the equation:

$$-P_d \times \left(1 + 0.75 \times \frac{8}{100}\right) \times \left(1 + \frac{8}{100}\right) + 5 \times \left(1 + 0.5 \times \frac{8}{100}\right) \times$$
$$\left(1 + \frac{8}{100}\right) + 5 \times \left(1 + \frac{8}{100}\right) + 5 \times \left(1 + 0.5 \times \frac{8}{100}\right) + 105 = 0$$

From which P_d is found to be 105.88.

The idea behind the Moosmüller method is similar to the Braess/Fangmeyer method except that interest on the account is compounded with the same frequency as coupon payments on the bond. Interest is credited to or debited from the account on coupon payment dates.

Formulae for the two methods are given below. The formulae apply to bonds without redemption schedules and part payment schedules, and which are redeemed on the final coupon date. The extension of the formulae to handle the more complicated cases is straightforward.

Moosmüller Formula

$$P_d \times \left(1 + \frac{Y_h}{100 \times H} \times K_1\right) = G_1' + G' \times \frac{(V - V^N)}{1 - V} + 100 \times V^{N-1}$$

**Braess/Fangmeyer
Formulae**

For bonds paying an annual coupon the Moosmüller and Braess/Fangmeyer methods are identical and the formula given above is used.

The general formulae for a semi-annual bond are given below. Different formulae need to be used depending on whether there is an even or odd number of coupon payments remaining.

In the formulae Y_a is the annually compounded yield and V_a is defined as:

$$V_a = \frac{1}{1 + \dfrac{Y_a}{100}}$$

N Even

$$P_d \times \left(1 + \frac{Y_a}{200} \times (1 + K_l)\right) = G' \times \left(2 + \frac{Y_a}{200}\right) \times \frac{(V_a - V_a^{N/2})}{(1 - V_a)} +$$

$$\left(1 + \frac{Y_a}{200}\right) \times G_i' + G' + 100 \times V_a^{N/2 - 1}$$

N Odd

$$P_d \times \left(1 + \frac{Y_a}{200} \times K_l\right) = G_i' + G' \times \left(2 + \frac{Y_a}{200}\right) \times$$

$$\frac{(V_a - V_a^{(N+1)/2})}{(1 - V_a)} + 100 \times V_a^{(N-1)/2}$$